327
F911

WITHDRAWN
SMU LIBRARIES

LIBRARY OF
Southern Methodist Univers

D1445733

FOREIGN POLICY IN THE MAKING

The Search for a New Balance of Power

LIBRARY OF
Southern Methodist University
DALLAS, TEXAS

The European Balance of Power

(FROM A LITHOGRAPH BY DAUMIER)

FOREIGN POLICY IN THE MAKING

The Search for a New Balance of Power

BY CARL JOACHIM FRIEDRICH

PROFESSOR OF GOVERNMENT, HARVARD UNIVERSITY

LIBRARY OF
Southern Methodist University
DALLAS, TEXAS

NEW YORK · W · W · NORTON & CO · INC.

Copyright, 1938, by
W. W. Norton & Company, Inc.
70 Fifth Avenue, New York City

FIRST EDITION

PRINTED IN THE UNITED STATES OF AMERICA

To the memory of my father
Paul Leopold Friedrich
† January 15, 1916

89357

Greater love hath no man than this, that a man lay down his life for his friends.

JOHN, 15:13

CONTENTS

FOREWORD

THE extended researches of which this book is a partial result were made possible by a grant from the Committee on International Research at Harvard University and Radcliffe College in 1931-32. At that time it was hoped to present a comparative study of the part parliaments were taking in the conduct of foreign affairs. The findings as well as the course of international events have rendered obsolete the original approach. The Committee has been generous and patient in its willingness to let the author work out his own and the world's salvation.

During recent years, a series of seminars on the politics of modern diplomacy at the Fletcher School of Law and Diplomacy have given the author a welcome opportunity to try out his conclusions in discussions with a select group of students. They have their share in molding my approach to these problems.

It is impossible to mention by name all the friends who have given aid and counsel during the years since I first commenced to explore the effect which our lumbering democratic ways are producing in the international sphere. I have indicated by a few references where the debt is clear. W. Y. Elliott has listened to and criticized my ideas as they developed. Rupert Emerson read and rejected an earlier manuscript—about four years ago. Alfred Vagts has commented upon the central problem of the balance of power in a particularly illuminating way. Last, but not least, Dr. Heinrich Brüning has read the entire manuscript and made helpful suggestions. The book probably would be better if I were as experienced as Dr. Brüning, as learned as Vagts, as idealist as Emerson, or as literary as Elliott—my thoughts cannot help but bear the mark of my several limitations.

For better or worse, the nature of political questions is such that no one can avoid a measure of subjective bias. If any reader should ever care to know what the framework of my preconceptions actually is he might look at *Constitutional Government and Politics—Its Nature and Development*. There I have tried to describe the way our democracies have traveled. This way shows, in spite of all the shortcomings of popular government, so bitterly felt at the moment, that we are still at the beginning and not at the end of its history. The present troubles are probably its measles, mumps, or scarlet fever. All government remains a disagreeable, at times even a shocking, concession to human frailty. Democracy continues to be the least objectionable of these connivances. Such is my belief, at least: many things in life are more valuable than order and government. Unfortunately, we cannot have them without order and government, because peace is difficult without order and government. Can we achieve peace by collaboration? Or must we eventually submit to one mighty Caesar? The following pages merely describe the failure of our efforts to achieve collaboration after the war.

Have the dead died in vain? The problem of a permanent peace has haunted me since as a boy I saw my mother widowed by the war. My father had been a good nineteenth-century nationalist, an admirer of Treitschke and the Empire. Yet he died helping friend and foe, a surgeon at the operating table saving as many lives as he could, until he collapsed from overwork. The paradox of his attitude and work seems to me the paradox of our own desire for peace. We want to gain it by fighting. How can it be? Let me acknowledge Kant's wisdom: only the triumph of constitutional government will bring us peace in permanency.

ONE

DEMOCRACY AND DICTATOR-SHIP IN FOREIGN AFFAIRS

The Ghosts of the Old Diplomacy

EVERYBODY in Europe expects war. Even Switzerland, proverbially pacific, is more and more martial in appearance. The streets are full of soldiers; with their heavy knapsacks and rifles they crowd the narrow platforms of the streetcars in Berne and Zürich and Bâle. As you ride through the beautiful valleys toward the Gotthard pass, big steel doors are pointed out to you at the foot of some of these giant mountains; they cover the entrance to huge caves which have been dug into the mountains for the storage of war materials. Down in the sunny Tessin, the Italian-speaking canton of Switzerland where at Locarno the conciliation treaties were concluded in 1925, everyone has his place assigned at the mountain passes and on the few highways to ward off an attack by Mussolini. . . . How could this happen? Has democracy utterly failed in the field of foreign affairs? Are we to go back to the "now forever discredited game of the balance of power"?

There are two countries in the world today which

11

have been democracies long enough to allow some perspective on their behavior in foreign affairs: the United States and Switzerland. Neither of them has shown much inclination to develop an active foreign policy. The watchword of Swiss foreign relations has been "neutrality," that of the United States "isolation." [1] Should we conclude that democratic countries shun a foreign policy? Is America, as Livingston Hartley has recently put it, simply afraid? There can be no question that both peoples have an ardent wish to be left alone. Our timid adventures into colonial imperialism are being liquidated. There is an overwhelming sentiment in the United States in favor of letting the Philippines have their independence if they want it, indeed, even if they do not. To be sure, Americans had few qualms over appropriating the continent. The pioneers created an empire, but all the frontiersmen remained an integral part of the American people. There were no colonials and the Indians were too few to count as a subject race.

The American past does not contain figures like Richelieu, Frederick of Prussia, Bismarck, or even Talleyrand. Those masters of the old diplomacy all played a game for which there was no room in a democracy. Are the conditions under which the American people and the Swiss people have built their institutions and developed their democratic way of life so peculiar to them that the rest of the world will be

---

[1] See Benjamin H. Williams, *American Diplomacy* (1936), Max Huber, *Die Schweizerische Neutralität und der Völkerbund* (1924), and Schweizer, *Geschichte der Schweizerischen Neutralität* (1895).

unable to follow their example? Or do their outlook and their behavior contain a universal precept? Certainly the conditions under which a democratic conduct of foreign affairs was attempted in Europe after the World War were very different from those in which the Swiss and Americans have found themselves during the last hundred years. Switzerland on account of her size, America on account of her remoteness, were unlikely to come into conflict with other powers. They themselves would have had to take an aggressive step. Not so the European democracies after the war. The map of Europe was their heritage from a monarchical past. The rival policies of the past haunted the New Europe.

Measured by the high expectations of its founders, the League of Nations has failed. Who is responsible? Was the ideal too grandiose, or were the policies of the statesmen too picayune? Here are questions of vital importance, a body of experience which should be assessed without delay. All kinds of prejudices have been feeding on it. Pessimists have cried, "I told you so," cynics have joined forces with armament manufacturers in asking, "What did you expect?" while the optimists have kept smiling through it all. Even if scientific conclusions cannot be reached, an examination of these complex happenings done with a measure of scholarly detachment should be attempted. Democracy needs science and faith in understanding our past mistakes. Its creed is built on the brave if painful learning by trial and error.

Nobody today believes that the mere organizing of

a League of Nations will bring about peace. Here, after all, is a tremendous gain, real progress toward understanding. But during the fifteen years between 1918 and 1933, all sorts of experiments were made to implement the international machinery of democratic collaboration. What do these experiments teach us? The most promising of these experiments is epitomized by the name Locarno. When Chamberlain, Briand, and Stresemann gathered around the table to discuss common problems, many believed that at long last the new era had dawned. The "spirit of Locarno" became a slogan of bright hope for international appeasement. But this spirit evaporated almost as quickly as the spirit of the Fourteen Points. Upon what rock did these hopes founder?

Dr. Eduard Beneš, level-headed internationalist that he is, stated the central difficulty as early as 1919. He had reason to face the facts, being then the Foreign Minister of Czechoslovakia, a small, newly created democratic government. Although a strong believer in the League, he was convinced that for some time to come world politics would be dominated by the problem of how to maintain an equilibrium between the nations and their governments. He felt sure that such a balance might be maintained under the League. But if it were not, the League would fail, and there would once more be a policy of coalitions and blocs. Wilson had not seen this clearly. Here is the clue to the problems which postwar diplomacy presents. How can an equilibrium be maintained between democratic nations? The people is supposed to be all-powerful in a democracy. But there are the French people, the German people, the English and the Italian people, all separate and distinct; what if their "sovereign" wills should clash? In the old times, one of the most dangerous events had been the meeting of two sovereign princes; diplomats trembled for weeks beforehand. Now sovereign peoples stood facing each other day in, day out. Their voices mingled disharmoniously, and feelings were easily hurt by the unrestrained language of extremists on all sides. Writers and speakers had not learned to restrain themselves, nor had the mass of the people acquired the tough skin which protects the partisan in a democracy against the abuse of his opponents. They kept alive the ghosts of the old diplomacy.

Democracy in Foreign Affairs Before the War

Is it not true that there was a good deal of democracy in prewar diplomacy? Was not the foreign policy of France and of England democratic? Yes and no. There were certainly those who, like M. Joseph-Barthélemy, would like to have us think so.[2] In both countries, a semiofficial propaganda maintained that the impending conflict would be one between democracy and autocracy. As long as you considered only France and Germany, this view had a semblance of truth. But Czarist Russia disturbed it, did not fit into this picture, any more than Stalinist Russia does today. Fortunately, people are not too much troubled by inconsistencies. Propagandists readily argued away any

[2] See his *Démocratie et Politique Etrangère* (1917).

logical objections. "Not affinity of political institutions, but solely the concordance of interests should determine alliances. French diplomacy should pursue exclusively the grandeur of France." To clinch the argument, the imposing memory of Richelieu was conjured up. All very well, except for the argument that it was a fight between democracy and autocracy.

To the detached student of these ominous years before the war, Europe appears to have been in a period of transition. Democracy was making steady gains. Even in countries like Russia, Austria-Hungary, and Japan, concessions to popular control were the order of the day. In Germany, democratic forces were surging behind the imposing imperial façade. The Big Navy policy was as much the result of broad popular pressures as of the Kaiser's sovereign will. In 1908 Prince Bülow fell from power, the scapegoat of a conflict between Emperor and Parliament. The constantly widening mass support for various kinds of progressivism heralded the dawn of a parliamentary era in German politics. In France, monarchical sentiment was completely in eclipse. After the *affaire Dreyfus* had, at the turn of the century, given a powerful impetus to all progressive parties, the Third Republic entered upon the serene era of "the republic of comrades" so brilliantly portrayed by de Jouvenel.[3]

In England, the rise of the Labor party meant that radically democratic groups were at long last roundly challenging the aristocratic tradition. When Keir Hardie refused to go to a Court reception in knee

[3] Robert de Jouvenel, *La République des Camarades* (1913).

breeches, the Empire seemed to rock on its foundations. Would these people be able to develop a foreign policy? The infrequent debates in the House of Commons showed them vigorous, at times even bitter, critics of British imperialism and of its diplomacy. But there was no clear indication as to what they themselves would do, if put into power. They demanded a parliamentary committee for foreign affairs to control British diplomacy. Just what sort of control could have been imposed, what foreign policy advocated, remains pure guesswork. There was a boundless faith in the people, its pacific nature and its common sense. Would the people be prepared to retrench and abandon the Empire?

Opposition to these democratic impulses remained dominant before the war in all the leading countries except America. The clamor of English Socialists for a real share in foreign affairs encountered stout resistance.[4] Their most poignant questions often remained unanswered. In France, where parliament had a small share in the direction of foreign affairs through its committee in both Senate and Chamber of Deputies,[5] such influence remained effectively insulated against popular pressures. In Germany, the weak position of the Reichstag only allowed it enough nuisance value to oblige the government to carry on extensive propaganda in support of its repeated demands for in-

[4] See William P. Maddox, *Foreign Relations in British Labour Politics* (1934).

[5] See Joseph-Barthélemy, *Essai sur le Travail Parlementaire,* 1934, ch. VIII.

creased army and navy budgets. These situations were paralleled elsewhere; indeed, they were in general the unhappy result of increased popular influence.

Evidently, the "irresistible progress of democracy" had not yet conquered foreign policy. The very limited impact of popular forces had upset the older balance of power without being able to build a new one to suit democracy's peculiar dynamics. A system of inflexible alliances developed. It was a period of rapid transition. The outbreak of the war stems clearly from the resulting confusion and uncertainty. And yet, how much more stable and orderly did the world appear in 1914 than it does today! The terrific clash of ideologies and interests in recent years almost gives the aura of a golden age to those portentous years before the World War. But we know, deep down in our hearts, that it was all a great illusion. European society was sick, if not moribund. A study of the diplomatic documents tells a sorry tale. Nothing is more disheartening than to retrace the doings of the weaklings who tried to conduct foreign policy without knowing how or why. Standing upon a great tradition, these men tried to govern a growing democratic society with the tools which monarchical and aristocratic statesmanship had forged to serve its imperialist purposes. Naturally, the tools did not work. A world war was the result, more formidable and all-inclusive than any war which had preceded it. Yet for what? When the several governments attempted to formulate their war aims, they fumbled. There were jingoists and imperialists aplenty who wanted this province or that colony, but there was no substantial support for any of these "purposes." They were invented after the event to justify a struggle which had no rhyme or reason at all.

War and Peace

The old diplomacy was developed during a time when wars were limited in scope. The French and American revolutions mark the beginning of a change. The *levée en masse* brought out the people in arms to defend the revolutions against reactionary intervention. From then on wars became increasingly comprehensive. Napoleon's campaigns continued the revolutionary tradition. The Prussians adapted it to their needs in preparation for the "wars of liberation." A steady progression since that time has brought us near the "totalitarian war." Such a war demands the participation of every man, woman, and child. Whether workers or capital resources, every bit of reserve must be brought forward to help the nation toward victory. The World War went a long way toward a total mobilization; since that time legislation in various countries has gone beyond it. It is puzzling that genuine pacifists often advocate such a total mobilization; the French bill was put through by Paul-Boncour, an ardent advocate of the League. The idea behind this bill is that everyone should be obliged to make sacrifices to the limit of his ability. War profiteers must be made impossible. "Make the absence of war more desirable for everyone, and war will not take place."

Unfortunately, the facts contradict this expectation. In his penetrating way, the philosopher Spinoza once suggested the difficulty of achieving real peace. "Peace," he said, "does not merely mean the absence of war, but the kind of goodness which is born of a strong spirit." [6] To tell people that they will all have to partake in the sacrifice does not create that strong spirit. Indeed, the ardor of many to sacrifice themselves for something or somebody is so great that the possibility of war may be increased. The fear of violent death is not nearly so great as Hobbes supposed, and is often far exceeded by the fear of boredom and by the nausea resulting from thwarted ambition. A feeling of strength can only be engendered by concentrating man's efforts upon deeply felt tasks of a creative kind. Not long ago, a philosophical wit concocted a utopia to cope with this difficulty. The leaders of the world, aware of man's longing to throw himself heart and soul into a great enterprise without regard for personal gain, had somehow managed to get all the people in Europe to participate frantically in the building of a second Mont Blanc. No doubt, there are plenty of tasks with which nature confronts us which are even more stupendous than building another Mont Blanc. But unless we succeed in concentrating man's fighting instincts upon these tasks by effectively dramatizing them, they will not hold the center of the stage. Who knows but that the vast draining enterprises of the Egyptian kings, or the building of the Great Wall by China's emperors, were at least in part serving the purpose of internal pacification?

[6] "Pax enim non belli privatio, sed virtus est, quae ex animi fortitudine oritur."

The peacemakers of 1919 had little sympathy with the vanquished; their spirit was far from strong. If they cherished some hope of building a lasting peace, they thought of it almost entirely in terms of banishing war. Could the time between wars, the mere absence of war, be accepted as peace in a democratic age? It is easy to see in retrospect that it could not. For the first time in history both the victors and the vanquished were peoples governing themselves. But neither of them was animated by the strong spirit. The victors were haunted by fear and suspicion; they could not trust those whom they knew they had mistreated. The vanquished were writhing in bitter humiliation; they could not forgive those who had defeated them. They refused to believe that they had been beaten. They invented the legend of the "stab in the back."

America and Wilson came perhaps nearest to the true spirit of peace; some noble Americans actually left the Paris Peace Conference and sailed home when they realized what was going to happen. But Wilson could not prevail. Indeed, he succumbed to the fears and animosities of the others. Democracy was, after all, only a frail young thing. Are we fair in expecting it to have succeeded at the first trial? There was altogether too much emphasis on organization and superstructure, too little on the underlying folkways. Democratic institutions were to function without any democratic way of life to give these institutions meaning and stability. The weakness of democracy was the weakness of the democratic union of the nations.

President Wilson's Initiative

In view of his failure to make a real peace, we are nowadays too prone to belittle the importance of Wilson's challenge. A wry smile of whimsical sympathy for his personal efforts—that is the best we feel we can do for him. Yet, the miscarriage of his efforts does not alter the fact that his call was a more significant act of democratic foreign policy than any which the United States had produced until that day. Washington's prudent counsel not to mix in the quarrels of Europe suggested the isolation which a democracy needed in a monarchical age. Monroe's doctrine was a sensible effort to keep these imperialist powers as far away from America as possible. The late colonial imperialism was a half-hearted attempt in an alien field. But through his Fourteen Points Wilson announced to the world the aspirations of democracy in the international sphere. It seems today a vague gesture, but as a first step it will stand. War weariness in Europe and a widespread democratic enthusiasm combined to provide a sounding board at the time. It is almost impossible today to recapture the spirit of hope which Wilson's redundant phrases aroused at the time.

A vigorous protest against the principle of the balance of power was a vital part of Wilson's message. There had been so much talk about this balance of power that the apostle of a new international order was bound to challenge the idea. "Peoples and provinces are not to be bartered about from sovereignty to sovereignty as if they were mere chattels and pawns in a game, even the great game, now forever discredited, of the balance of power; but every territorial settlement involved in this war must be made in the interest and for the benefit of the populations concerned and not as a part of any mere adjustments or compromise of claims among rival states." [7] A League of Nations was to be substituted for this iniquitous game of the balance of power. The arguments are only too familiar. The balance of power was held to be responsible for the unstable conditions which had resulted in the disaster of the World War. Was it not also to blame for the partition of Poland? And closely connected with it was the system of secret alliances. Equilibrium and secret diplomacy were symbols of the sparring for position by which the European powers had always sought to buttress their ill-gotten gains.

To all those who had faith in these proclamations those days appeared like a turning point in history. Was the new gospel not an extension of the spirit which brought about the founding of the United States? Then, as now, unity through federal union had been the solution of the conflicts of local prejudice and interest. It was the democratic answer to the recurrent autocratic bid for universal empire. Rather facetiously, William II was pictured as a successor to Napoleon I, Louis XIV, and Charles V. He, like them, was represented as only checked by balance of power diplomacy. In retrospect, it seems like excessive flattery, but at the

[7] *The Messages and Papers of Woodrow Wilson,* New York, 1924, I, 478. This is one of the four supplementary principles, not one of the original Fourteen Points.

time, most people believed that the Kaiser had started the World War to achieve universal empire. With the collapse of autocracy in Russia, Germany, and Austria-Hungary, the victory of democracy seemed assured. Clearly, the day had come to found an eternal and universal peace through the establishment of an equitable international order.

A federation of free nations was to displace both balance of power and universal empire. Had not the centuries since the decline of the Holy Roman Empire given birth to many dreams for such a federation? The *Grand Dessein* of Henry IV of France was conceived in 1610 to counteract the Hapsburgs' claim to universal empire; the Abbé Saint-Pierre's *Projet pour rendre la Paix perpetuelle en Europe* appeared between 1713 and 1717 after Louis XIV had sought supremacy; Immanuel Kant's *Essay on Eternal Peace* in 1795 anticipated an answer to Napoleon's imperial ambitions. The time seemed to have come for the realization of these dreams. It is the grandeur of Wilson to have had the courage to voice this faith.

The Communist Challenge

Before Wilson ever spoke, a challenging appeal for making mankind into a federal union of free peoples had already gone out. Just a month or so before Wilson formulated his Fourteen Points, the Communists had taken over the government in Russia. The Union of Soviet Socialist Republics was intended to be universal and international in scope.

Since 1847, the Communist Manifesto had called

upon the workers of the world to unite. The prewar days had seen the building of an international federation of Socialist parties. This *Internationale* had been shattered by the outbreak of the war. There were some remnants of it in Holland, Switzerland, and the Scandinavian countries. These had endeavored, in 1917, to bring the World War to an end. A bold dream. Had it succeeded it might have forestalled the radicalization of the Russian masses which gave the Bolsheviks the upper hand. But the obstruction of the embattled governments had thwarted these efforts. Samuel Gompers had denounced it as a Prussian intrigue. Frightened lest the fighting morale of their people be undermined by active participation of some of their leaders in a conference, England and France had refused passports.[8]

By the beginning of 1918, Socialists everywhere were turning away from the idea of international reform. Nothing short of a world revolution seemed to promise eternal peace. Imperialist governments, whether democratic or autocratic, would never banish the scourge of war. Communists and Socialists alike scoffed at a federation of such governments; though dressed up as a League of *Nations,* it would turn out to be an alliance of imperialist *governments* seeking to destroy the emerging workers' international union. The defiant grandeur envisaged by these radical dreamers was dramatically expressed by the new constitution of the Union of Soviet Socialist Republics. It makes as strange

[8] See the admirable study by Merle Fainsod, *The Origin of the Third International,* 1935.

reading today, after the Stalinist purges, as do the Fourteen Points. But it stands as a permanent challenge, just as they do.

"To all governments and to all peoples of the earth: From the first moment of their existence the Soviet Republics were united by the bonds of close co-operation and mutual assistance. . . . The solidarity of the laboring masses united them in their common task of establishing fraternal co-operation between the liberated peoples. . . . This union of peoples with equal rights remains a purely voluntary union which excludes all possibility of national oppression or the compulsion of any nation to remain within this united state, every republic enjoying the right to leave the republic if it so desires. At the same time the door is left open for the voluntary entry into the union of other socialist republics that may be formed in the future." [9]

Three Principles of Diplomacy

There are several ways in which one might study the complications which arose in connection with democratic diplomacy after the war. An outright diplomatic history would reveal a good deal, but there is not yet sufficient documentary material available for more than an impressionistic account.[10] Studies of international relations are significant, and many good ones have been written, among them the striking annual *Survey of International Affairs* by Arnold Toynbee.

[9] This translation is taken from W. R. Batsell, *Soviet Rule in Russia,* 1929. See also E. Pashukanis, *Ten Years of the USSR Constitution,* 1933.

[10] The two studies by Harold Nicolson, *Peacemaking 1919* and *Lord Curzon, The Third Phase,* are rather significant case studies to which more detailed reference will be made later.

Parliamentary influence upon the conduct of foreign affairs offers an interesting line of attack.[11] Instead of following any of these approaches, this study attempts to outline the pattern of democratic foreign policy in postwar Europe by asking what changes it has brought about in certain time-honored rules or principles according to which diplomacy was supposed to be conducted in former days. These rules are not high ideals through which an ethical conception of international affairs might exert what influence it can upon the brute reality. Rather they seek to explain and teach what rules of conduct have through trial and error been found to be sound and expedient.

Of these "principles," that of the balance of power or of the equilibrium of power is the most famous. It suggests, in its simplest form, that governments should seek to forestall the continuous expansion of any other government by balancing its power through suitable counteralliances. The reason given for this rule is that such expansion threatens the very existence of the weaker governments. Dr. Beneš's opinion cited before is clearly based upon this idea. Since the maintenance of an independent existence is posited as the foremost objective of all foreign policy, the crucial importance of such a principle, if sound, can readily be seen. Just what it might mean within the context of the League, only an examination of the postwar experience can show.

[11] See Frederick L. Schuman, *War and Diplomacy in the French Republic,* 1931, and Francis R. Flournoy, *Parliament and War,* 1927. More comprehensive and comparative in scope is D. C. Poole, *The Conduct of Foreign Relations under Modern Democratic Conditions,* 1924.

The second principle is likewise riveted upon the supreme task of maintaining the existence of the state. It teaches that considerations of foreign policy should outweigh considerations of domestic policy because international complications might threaten the very existence of the body politic. But what of the popular will? Are not the people apt to prefer domestic to international issues? How can the two be distinguished under modern conditions anyway? In these questions lies the crux of an analysis of the second principle.

The third principle is related to the second. It claims that foreign policy ought to be continuous in order to be effective: a vacillating policy is worse than no policy at all. Yet, are not the people divided into parties alternating in office? Do not these parties hold different views of foreign policy which they will attempt to carry out when they come into power? Just think of Conservatives and Labor in England, their clash over relations to Russia, over international collective security, and so on. The issue is distinct and well defined.

These three principles—of the balance of power, of the greater weight of foreign policy, and of continuity —were worked out under the conditions of monarchical foreign policy. Are they still workable rules under democratic conditions? If not, what changes have taken place? What further change may be expected as a consequence of democracy in foreign affairs? It will be shown that each one of the three principles is profoundly affected by democracy. It should, of course, be remembered that these rules were often violated. Autocratic foreign policy vacillated often enough, being vitiated by domestic and dynastic prejudices. An equilibrium was never achieved for any length of time. Yet none of these rules is inherently incompatible with an authoritarian government. Before the advent of democracy, their infringement was due to human frailty, not to conflict of principle. It is only when such conflicts occur that the coming of a new order is heralded.

Fascism Reasserts the Old Principles

Democracy has had a lot of trouble in trying to develop new methods. Many people in Europe have lost all patience. Let us go back, they have shouted. Fascism is the result, and so is Nazism. Do these authoritarian revivals really show a way out? Do they serve the national interest in whose pursuit they continuously celebrate victories? These are urgent questions; for those who despair of democracy have taken refuge in such views.

Everyone knows that the present crisis of democracy has been brought about by the aggravation of two bitter conflicts. There is the internal conflict between capital and labor which, it is claimed, necessitates a strong government to enforce compromises in the public interest to prevent civil war. There is also the supposed failure of democracy in international affairs, its inclination to sacrifice the "national" interest: international conflicts demand a more effective concentration of national leadership, so the Fascist legend goes. The idea of national interest, to be sure, is a thoroughly democratic concept.[12] But the democratic process with its all too apparent perennial cockfights between various parties and pressure groups undermines the confidence of the public. It suggests that the national interest is being neglected and even jeopardized. Men of veracity and strenuous devotion to ideals appear who make vigorous attacks upon the general corruption. Their Cassandra-like warnings operate as a leaven; after fermentation has begun, the Hitlers, Mussolinis, and their ilk commence to exploit the widespread popular discontent and ill-feeling.

Foreign affairs play an important part in these developments. The mass of the people are unfamiliar with the difficulties confronting the government. It is relatively easy to create the impression that every compromise is the result of sloth and cowardice—a wanton sacrifice of justified national claims. Demagogues minimize the claims of other peoples. After the war, such appeals were easy in Germany, since no government could hope to redress the situation rapidly enough to appease the popular indignation aroused by the treaty settlement. What was true of Germany was to a lesser extent true of Austria, Hungary, Italy. Nor can it be denied that the policy of these more or less recently established democratic governments was often hesitant, pusillanimous, unsteady.

In the League of Nations, supposed to have taken the place of the balance of power, these weaker governments found themselves overshadowed by the English

[12] See Charles A. Beard, *The Idea of National Interest*, 1934, particularly ch. I. See also the discussion below, pp. 95 ff.

and the French. Having been the victors in the war, the English and French were suspected of utilizing the League for maintaining themselves in power. The French presumably exchanged British acceptance of French hegemony in Europe for French recognition of British hegemony in other parts of the world. The League thus seemed to be a strait jacket put upon weak governments to make the strong stronger, instead of balancing their power and pretensions through suitable alliances. Dictatorship by a bureaucratic elite seemed by contrast to promise chances for regaining part of the lost national power and prestige, or for acquiring a much desired imperial sway. A dictatorial regime might defy the League, or play hide-and-seek with it, as seemed best under varying circumstances, without fear of internal opposition from believers in the League. Similarly, it could give back to foreign policy its precedence over all domestic concerns by eliminating the conflicts of party and the meddling of public opinion. Finally, it could pursue a continuous, steady policy, undisturbed by changes in popular preference and fashion. There was a time when even thoughtful friends of democracy were inclined to wonder whether a policy of peace might not rest more securely upon Fascist foundations. The glorification of war as an heroic occasion continued to lurk behind all such policy, however. Peace on such terms remained a truce during which to prepare for the eventual armed conflict.

Fascism—the Reality

Actually, the record of these "dictatorial" regimes is quite different from their theory. Far from remov-

PREPARATIFS

COMITÉ DE NON-INTERVENTION

(JEAN EFFEL IN LE CANARD ENCHAÎNÉ)

Put the Non-Carafe upon the Non-Table . . .

ing foreign policy from the gusts of popular passion, international affairs are made into the red flag perpetually to be waved in front of the populace. Dictators may be dictating to individuals and small groups of the people, but they are positively servile when it comes to the masses. On certain occasions, nothing short of some such term as "mobocracy" would effectively characterize their methods. "Victories" in the field of foreign affairs appear to be the last straw which these governments turn to every time their hold becomes shaky.

"The meaning of such a consultation of the people by the Leader is to be seen in the fact that the relation of confidence between the Leader and the people as followers receives tangible political expression . . . ," so one Nazi authority tells us. Hitler has been strikingly successful in employing popular plebiscites for the purpose of demonstrating a united front in support of the aggressive foreign policy of the government. When Hitler, in the fall of 1933, decided to quit the League of Nations and the Disarmament Conference, he appealed to the German people to sanction this act. The move was meant to demonstrate to the whole world that this demand for "equality of treatment" was backed by the entire electorate. Doubtless there was widespread popular support for it. Yet, we know that the decision to make this move was made by Hitler only after many anxious consultations during which the obvious international disadvantages were weighed against the disadvantages of risking a further alienation of Hitler's own radical following. Anyone familiar with the internal situation could feel, during the summer of 1933, the deep antagonism and distrust which Hitler's failure to challenge the League had aroused in these radicalized masses. This is not to say that Hitler personally disagreed with them; quite the contrary. But the Foreign Office did; they urged Hitler not to take this step. The mob pressures prevailed; they forced the decision. It is important for any student of contemporary international affairs to keep this "popular pressure" behind dictatorial foreign policy constantly in mind.

A "consultation" also provides an occasion on which the lukewarm followers and the opponents of the regime are subjected to a barrage of nationalist propaganda in an effort to bring them into line behind the government. Since during those weeks of frenzied agitation nothing but government propaganda is dinned into the ears of the masses, they tend to swing into line and are thus assimilated by the radical party elements. In short, these dictatorial regimes are subject to emotional mass pressure, the most dangerous force generated by democracy in foreign affairs, yet they are entirely devoid of the restraining influence of an effective opposition. This has been true time and again. When Hitler reoccupied the Rhineland in the spring of 1936, he immediately proceeded to appeal to the German masses, as he had done in the previous year when announcing German rearmament in defiance of the Treaty of Versailles. In both cases popular support did not fail to come forth in impressive and compact numbers. Hitler's international antagonists were stunned and recoiled from forceful measures in the face of his solid national support. At critical moments in the life of the Nazi dictatorship one may, therefore, always look for some bold action in the international sphere, with a plebiscite following it to reintegrate the crumbling mass support. It is a technique which the Napoleons, as well as Cromwell, have practiced before.

The limited supply of safe outlets for that tendency augurs ill for the dictators as well as for Europe. At any rate, such craving for "victories" violently interferes with the techniques of the older diplomacy.

Neither the balance of power nor the precedence of foreign over domestic policy is truly a principle guiding dictatorial diplomacy. As for continuity, only the martial spirit seeking national aggrandizement is ever present, but the frantic search for suitable occasions to indulge in it entails a constantly shifting pattern of concrete policies which is bewildering. The impression that dictatorial regimes mark a return to the methods of the older diplomacy is quite superficial.

The Referendum—a Conclusion?

Mass emotionalism is the most dangerous force generated by democracy in foreign affairs. Macaulay once wrote to an American congressman that on account of it democracy would deliver every country with a foreign policy into the hands of a dictator within ten years after it had been established. That, of course, was an exaggeration born of the fear of the mob which the liberal aristocrat instinctively felt. Still, nobody would question today the terrific strains which mass nationalism has created throughout the world. How, then, is it possible that a proposal has been made and ardently supported for submitting the declaration of war to a popular referendum in the United States?

There can be no doubt that those who have advocated such an arrangement are animated by a deep desire to "keep America out of war." But the means which they have chosen are likely to make it more certain that the United States will be plunged into war. Here is the amendment to the Constitution proposed by Representative Ludlow:

"Except in the event of an invasion of the United States or its territorial possessions and attack upon its citizens residing therein, the authority of Congress to declare war shall not become effective until confirmed by a majority of all the votes cast thereon in a nation-wide referendum. Congress when it deems a national crisis to exist may by concurrent resolution refer the question of war and peace to the citizens of the United States, the question to be voted on being 'Shall the United States declare war on —?' . . ."

Now quite apart from the military and naval objections which may possibly be eliminated by suitable changes,[13] there remain two decisive political objections which cannot be eliminated, because they are inherent in the referendum as such. Switzerland, which has a referendum procedure, does not need to worry about them, because she is completely neutralized. Whether such neutrality is possible for the United States is an open question. It is not possible as long as the United States has foreign possessions, maintains the Monroe Doctrine, or in any other way expects to participate in the shaping of international policy.

As long as the United States is not completely neutralized, that is, as long as war remains a possibility, the first political objection is that a nation on the brink

[13] See the letter by former Secretary of State Stimson printed in the Appendix, and the debate in Congress.

of war ought to be, needs to be, united as far as possible. If a referendum is held, a partisan spirit is bound to associate itself with the issue and produce a dangerous split. If the war party loses (as the proponents of the referendum, of course, *hope* it will) nothing would prevent the government, nothing could prevent the government, after some further incidents from holding a second referendum. In the meantime public agitation could be further increased. The entry of America into the last war, often cited by friends of the referendum plan, shows this very clearly. For Wilson's re-election was in effect a referendum on this issue. "He kept us out of war!" was Wilson's slogan in the campaign. Yet, when a year later he sought congressional support for a declaration of war, he was given an overwhelming majority. He probably would have got a majority of the electorate. At the same time, the referendum would have revealed a broad division wholly inimical to the country's interest at the time.

The foregoing reflections lead to the other objection, which is really more fundamental and conclusive. The student of foreign affairs and propaganda cannot help feeling that a referendum provision simply means that every time an administration is approaching a war-threatening situation, it will build up a martial spirit in anticipation of the referendum. The public will be exposed to most of the pressures of war propaganda, even before there is a war. This will greatly heighten the danger of its coming about. In fact, from this standpoint such a referendum is about the most dangerous thing imaginable; it would turn every chance of war into a probability.

The political dynamics of large groups of people is curious. Having adopted a referendum, they tend to consider the problem of war and peace solved. They are lulled to sleep about the whole matter. In this respect the referendum proposal is comparable to the Briand-Kellogg Pact. Then as now everybody knew that things were going from bad to worse, yet nobody was ready to do anything about it. Since we still feared war, we all proceeded to celebrate our pacific intentions in an elaborate ceremonial. We denounced war as an instrument of national policy and got—wars without a declaration of war. Cynics have already grinned and suggested that the Ludlow amendment would merely make the United States go to war without declaring it. That may be overstating a good point. But because we do not want war, and yet know that it may be "necessary" or "unavoidable," we simply take refuge in providing for a consultation of the oracle—the American people. That done, we need have no qualm. "The war is right and godly. No doubt of it. The oracle has spoken. Conscientious objectors are not only cowards and unpatriotic, they are enemies of God."

Democracy as a form of government has not gone far in developing suitable techniques in the field of foreign affairs. Since its keyword is co-operative action, there can be reasonable assurance that democracies will struggle on toward methods for organizing such co-operative action among nations. Democracies are bound to seek for the establishment of a reign of law so that change can be brought about by counting heads rather than breaking them, internationally as well as nationally. But first efforts in this direction seem to have resulted in the breakdown of what little law there was in the relations between nations. We seem, indeed, to be back where we were before Hugo Grotius and his contemporaries sought to lay the intellectual foundations of an international order of some sort. With Henry L. Stimson we believe that such a reign of law "will begin with the co-operative action of those nations which, like ourselves, have already become habituated to the practice of self-government at home and self-control abroad." The following chapters are devoted to analyzing the great obstacles encountered on that path. They suggest that the democracies themselves have a long way to travel before they will be "organized for peace." This inquiry also suggests that nothing is more likely to thwart all hope of achieving this goal than a self-satisfied assumption that democracy at home insures peace abroad.

TWO

THE ROLE OF THE PEOPLE IN FOREIGN AFFAIRS

The People Desire Peace

THE man in the street the world over does not want to go to war. Women do not want their husbands, sons, and brothers to go to war, either. There are exceptions, of course. Spartan mothers and Roman matrons are proverbial for their martial spirit. Almost all nations have passed through periods when the struggle for freedom against foreign or domestic foes made men and women discard all personal sentiments. In their effort to build up a willingness for self-sacrifice, our contemporary tyrannies have through incessant propaganda stirred up combative inclinations amongst the people over which they rule. But even in these benighted lands many people, if not an actual majority, remain unmoved by the spell of official oratory. During Mussolini's Ethiopian campaign, voices of discontent could be heard throughout Italy, and it is often alleged that failure in the campaign would have meant certain disaster for the Fascist regime. Hitler, with his unlimited capacity for self-contradiction, feels impelled to intersperse his aggressive assertions with occasional fervent pleas for universal peace. It would be wrong to think that these are only for foreign consumption. For, even in Germany, most people do not want to go to war. When Hitler says: "No new European war could improve the unsatisfactory conditions of the present day," they are relieved. Everywhere, then, the common people prefer not to go to war. One might even go further and say that in this negative sense, the people desire peace. But this desire is unhappily very often the desire to eat one's cake and have it too.

The People Want Many Things Which Cause War

War and strife result from conflicts between nations over irreconcilable interests. Both England and Germany wanted supremacy in world trade, both France and Germany wanted Alsace-Lorraine, both Russia and Austria-Hungary wanted the hegemony of the Balkans; everybody knows that it is from claims such as these that wars arise. In a more poetic age, it was Helen of Troy, or Cleopatra, or Crimalda. Epic dramatization well depicts the human, emotional root of such conflicts. "The people" are prone to cherish any and all such interests with alacrity. They do not want to go to war, but they do want all that any ambitious rabble-rouser tells them they ought to have. They rival Hitler's capacity for self-contradiction, for they are human.

Democracy, so the doctrine claims, is government according to the will of the people. Whatever the people want, they are entitled to get or to do. It is a doctrine expounded by men who insist that they have the people's own concerns in mind. It has been preached as an antidote to government by and in favor of the privileged classes. As such it has been sound. But what is to happen if two such peoples, two such democracies, confront each other? If they both want the same thing? How is a compromise to be reached in such a situation? There are those who would reply that all that is necessary is to keep the *status quo* intact, to respect the sanctity of existing arrangements, and leave everything as it is. Such voices are less predominant at the moment, but they persist. It is a radical solution, but no doubt a solution. For what the people have once consented to, they ought not to abrogate except by agreement. Unfortunately, the more one-sided the *status quo,* the less likely the agreement.

In 1839 the Dutch and Belgians agreed to a settlement concerning the river Scheldt, as part of an international treaty sanctioning the separation of Belgium from Holland, according to which the Dutch were to have the river, but subject to the obligation to canalize it to a depth then allowing sea-going vessels to go up the river as far as Antwerp. The obvious intent was to safeguard the trade of Antwerp against discrimination by the Dutch through their control of the mouth of the river. The revolution in modern navigation has rendered these provisions utterly inadequate; yet an equitable agreement has not been worked out, and when a far-sighted Dutch statesman, van Karnebeek, attempted to negotiate such a settlement, he was defeated by an outburst of nationalist propaganda. This instance from a relatively neutral sector of international politics serves to show that there is only a difference in degree between the determined popular support for schemes involving the taking of what someone else possesses, and the even more determined popular insistence upon keeping all that a particular nation has got. Indeed, this is no isolated instance; illustrations could be multiplied by examples from the foreign policy of practically every power, including the United States. Our insistence upon the interallied debts is not in keeping with our pacific policy.

The Advocates of Popular Influence Have Failed to Take Account of the Complexity of Popular Pressures

Many of those who indiscriminately demanded the extension of democracy into the field of foreign affairs assumed that the popular desire for peace in the negative sense just described would readily shape itself into a policy for maintaining peace. Being themselves rationally-minded optimists, they seem to have felt that the people would readily abandon specific national claims once they discovered that these claims conflicted with the interests of other peoples. This hope was perhaps not wholly unfounded. Particularly within the Socialist groups of prewar Europe one finds a noticeable inclination toward real sacrifice. No one can read the speeches of Jean Jaurès in the French Chamber before the war without being moved by the genuine spirit of conciliation which they breathe. As opposed to the aggressive vindictiveness of the Clemenceaus, Poincarés, and their sort who were following the admonition of Gambetta regarding Alsace-Lorraine—never to speak of it, always to think of it—he demanded an internationally supervised plebiscite to discover the popular preference in these provinces. This is not the place in which to consider the practicability of such a proposal, which was as fiercely opposed by the German as by the French nationalists. It merely serves to illustrate the existence of a genuinely pacific spirit in certain quarters. Socialist opinion was inclined toward such compromise, of course, because it was thinking in terms of an emerging international community.

Even in Socialist quarters, there were many whose readiness to compromise stopped short of their own immediate interests. The dock workers in England, though good Socialists, would not hear of disarmament. Throughout Europe, the majority of Socialists voted the money necessary for the conduct of the war, weeping crocodile tears, hiding their faces behind the formulas of national propaganda. The French Socialists claimed to defend French republican and democratic ideals against German imperialism and autocracy; the German Socialists in turn alleged the defense of German Socialism and culture against the barbarism of Russian Czardom. American workers readily responded to the call to make the world safe for democracy. Such was the lukewarm support Socialists gave to policies necessitating genuine sacrifice of national interests; outside their ranks the solidarity of national support for national interests was and remains practically unimpaired. It seems incomprehensible today that men of great perspicacity and political experience should have been willing to trust to education as a means of overcoming these national proclivities.

Education Is Insufficient

Education is an impotant part of the democratic process. But even if all education could be geared to awakening in all the people a sense of responsibility toward foreign affairs, it is doubtful whether it could successfully combat the effects of incessant propaganda. The German Republican constitution voiced one of its noblest aspirations when it provided that in all schools civics should be taught "in the spirit of German traditions and of international conciliation." Do not these two spirits contradict each other? Leading constitutional lawyers in Germany thought they did not. "National sentiment and honour not only permits, but demands an understanding for the sentiments of other nations. Such understanding is a condition for international conciliation. Another condition is equality, the mutual recognition of sovereignty. How deeply the Treaty of Versailles violates this principle is too well-known. . . . It cannot be the intention of this article to forbid the teacher to call the attention of the pupils to such inequalities."

Whether we sympathize with such views or not, it is clear that education will be slow in eradicating the source of international conflicts, deeply rooted as they are in conflicts of interest and point of view, even when education is conceived in a conciliatory spirit. In fact, as everyone knows, patrioteers are at work everywhere to have education, and particularly elementary education, devoted to exactly the opposite task. The teacher in schools and colleges is urged to extol the superiority of national institutions and traditions, to inculcate hero-worship for the great men of the national past, even if not to sow hatred for other nations. If all educators acted differently, there would still be the overwhelming influence of the home. At the suggestion of Charles E. Merriam, a group of scholars some time ago made a survey of the forces contributing toward the making of citizens in various countries. They found much evidence substantiating the general impression that education cannot easily be diverted to the task of promoting international solidarity because it has so important a function in developing civic loyalty. National political solidarity depends upon it. After surveying the facts, Merriam has concluded: "The fact is that in all cases [of contemporary political systems] the school system is the basic factor in the development of civic interest and loyalty, and the chief instrument for that purpose. . . . In the scheme of civic education it looms largest in the series of techniques employed to develop civic feeling and allegiance."[1] The nationalist outlook in foreign affairs provides too convenient a help in these efforts to be readily given up by educators in a democracy.

[1] Charles E. Merriam, *The Making of Citizens* (1931).

Democracies Have not Been Organized to Deal with Foreign Affairs

Once the vague hope for a pacific policy built upon the desire of the people at large not to go to war has proved to be an illusion, one is faced with a blank. Popular governments simply are not organized to cope with the problems which arise in their dealings with foreign powers. This is entirely natural. The primary impulse toward democratization sprang from a desire to mend internal politics, more particularly in the field of social reform. The irresistible march of democracy, as one contemporary author has called this process, resounded to the step of the battalions of the common people, especially the industrial workers. Its explicit endeavors were aimed at the abolition of privilege, the spread of equality of opportunities for everyone as individuals. Foreign affairs went by default.

It is surely no accident that the greatest apostle of equalitarian democracy, Jean-Jacques Rousseau, gainsaid the importance of foreign affairs. "What matters principally to every citizen," he wrote in 1764, heralding the French Revolution, "is the observance of the laws internally, the maintenance of private property and the security of the individual. As long as all goes well with regard to these three points, let the government [*les conseils*] negotiate and make treaties with foreign powers. It is not from this quarter that the dangers will come which are most to be feared." How unsound this advice was, the course of the French Revolution soon showed. A few years after the establishment of the Republic, Napoleon was dictator-emperor of the French, having risen to power as the military defender of revolutionary France against foreign invasions.

More recently, the German revolutionaries of 1918, though they conceived their constitutional democracy as "inspired by the determination to renew and strengthen their commonwealth in liberty and justice, to preserve peace both at home and abroad, and to foster social progress," were forced to admit the supremacy of the Treaty of Versailles in a concluding paragraph. The provisions of the Treaty being what they were, this humiliation in the field of foreign affairs soon proved again how easily a government will be destroyed by disasters abroad. Indeed, the catastrophes in which medieval constitutionalism became embroiled in the course of the sixteenth and seventeenth centuries gave rise to the very governments against which Rousseau and the early prophets of democracy were fighting. Masterful princes had become supreme because they alone seemed to offer a way out of the horrors of civil and foreign war.

The makers of the American Constitution were aware of the dangers which lurk in foreign affairs. Having won independence through the sword they appreciated the crucial significance of foreign policy. Benjamin Franklin's skilled diplomacy at the French Court had, as everyone knew, kept the French monarchy from joining forces with the British in suppressing a revolutionary movement which heralded its own doom. Eventually the French had even come to the financial support of the American revolutionaries.

This realization is nowhere so clearly evident as in the *Federalist,* of which the first five papers are entirely devoted to a discussion of the dangers "from foreign force and influence." Jay, who wrote these papers, did not share the illusionist views concerning popular influence in foreign affairs. He wrote: "It is true, however disgraceful it may be to human nature, that nations in general will make war whenever they have a prospect of getting anything by it." He then proceeded to elaborate upon some of the potential sources of conflict. These considerations were given much weight in the later papers dealing with the Senate, probably written by Madison. Whatever one may think of the arguments based on "the propensity of all single and numerous assemblies to yield to the impulse of sudden and violent passions, and to be seduced by factious leaders into intemperate and pernicious resolutions," the history of the last score of years has given ample proof of the cogency of such reflections in international affairs.

Whether the American Senate has served the purpose of coping with these difficulties or not—and we must not forget that the present Senate is no longer what the makers of the Constitution intended it to be: a small body capable of functioning as an executive body—it is unquestionable that the architects of the American government realized the danger and intended that it should be met. They were much concerned also with the disadvantages which would arise from an unstable, discontinuous policy, because such a policy would be detrimental to the best interests of the country, partly because it would undermine the confidence of foreign powers (as it already had when they wrote). They wisely argued that frequent elections would produce irresponsibility in matters resulting "from the mixed transactions of several years." A more stable body, elected indirectly, would be more responsible and "sometimes necessary as a defense to the people against their own temporary errors and delusions . . . ; there are particular moments in public affairs when the people, stimulated by some irregular passion, or some illicit advantage, or misled by the artful misrepresentations of interested men, may call for measures which they themselves will afterwards be the most ready to lament and condemn." This is not to argue against democracy, for "the cool and deliberate sense of the community . . . will, in all free governments, ultimately prevail over the views of its rulers."

Unhappily the changes in the composition of the Senate have rendered nugatory the "intention of the framers." The Senate today is not the body to which these arguments apply, for it is three times as large, and directly elected by the people. Therefore, the United States no longer possesses the institutional safeguards in foreign affairs which originally were provided for by men who fully realized the dependence of government upon the skillful conduct of foreign affairs.[2]

---

[2] W. Y. Elliott, in his *The Need for Constitutional Reform,* has rightly argued that a smaller Senate such as would result from his proposals would mean a return to these safeguards.

Versailles

The fatal incapacity of democracies in foreign affairs has become apparent to all who have reflected upon the making of peace after the World War. Patently, democracies proved unable to bring about genuine pacification. Politicians found themselves confronted with an unprecedented situation. The passion and furor which had been whipped up by wartime propaganda—a propaganda built upon infamous slanders too revolting to recall—simply would not subside. Everywhere the supposed "leaders" of the people found themselves the captives of their own past. Stirred by the revengeful imagination of a Northcliffe, or a Kipling, the English public began to resound with phrases like "Hang the Kaiser" and "Let us squeeze the orange till the pips squeak." Similar views were widely held in America, and even more violent and bitter feelings predominated in France. People engaged in mutual recriminations and moral indignation. Nor is there any doubt but that the German public would have displayed precisely the same spirit; indeed, the Treaty of Brest-Litovsk provides clear evidence for this contention.

It is obviously not a question of this or that nation. We are facing here a general *malaise* of popular government. It must be studied, in order to be properly diagnosed and treated. For there can be little doubt that some of the worst features of the Versailles settlement are clearly related to this popular pressure. The actual total of reparation payments was left undecided, and thus allowed to ruin German credit and to poison international relations for years to come. The possible sums fell so far short of the exaggerated expectations of the believers in *"les boches paieront"* and of the orange-squeezers that neither Clemenceau nor Lloyd George dared to set down any figures. Again, the justification for huge indemnities had to be found in the clause declaring Germany's sole responsibility for the outbreak of the war. This added insult to injury, and provided a mainspring for a violent nationalist reaction in Germany. There is little to be gained by further enumerating the many provisions of the Treaty which were included against the better judgment of the responsible politicians and hence may in one way or another be traced to mass pressure. How did this mass pressure actually work?

The Khaki Election in England

Almost immediately after the conclusion of the Armistice, Lloyd George, the Prime Minister of a coalition cabinet, called a general election. This general election, known as the Khaki or Coupon Election, was held in December. Mr. H. H. Asquith deplored it as "both a blunder and a calamity." Harold Nicolson, in his *Peacemaking 1919,* comments that "it was certainly a disaster: it is questionable whether it was also a mistake." It was a calamity and a disaster because "it returned to Westminster the most unintelligent body of public-school boys which even the Mother of Parliaments has known." Yet Nicolson would rather call it a regrettable necessity than a mistake, and supports this contention by the following argument.

"The Coalition Government were menaced at the moment by conspiracies both from the right and from the left. The former, headed by that ego-maniac, Lord Northcliffe, were all for a peace of victors. The latter, backed by a fierce tide of ignorant opinion, were clamoring for immediate demobilization. Had Lloyd George proceeded to Paris with both his flanks thus continually exposed, he would have been hampered in his every decision. It was essential for him to provide himself with an unassailable mandate. Clearly he could not have foreseen that his coupon election would saddle him with a House of Commons so unintelligent as to become subservient to such ill-balanced persons as Colonel Claude Lowther and Mr. Kennedy Jones." "Nor was this all. Mr. Lloyd George foresaw that if he were to cope adequately with the tortured nationalism of France, with the mystic and arrogant republicanism of America, and with the potential disunity of the Dominion Delegations, he would need to render his own *representative* quality assured beyond all possible challenge."

So much for Lloyd George and Harold Nicolson. The argument essentially turns upon two points: that Lloyd George could not have foreseen the outcome of the election, and that he must make himself unassailably representative. Let us examine these contentions.

The Khaki Election Was a Mistake

Did Lloyd George become unassailably representative by a majority in Parliament which, while formally supporting him, was actually entirely opposed to his policies? The answer can best be deduced from the taciturnity of the Prime Minister in Parliament, as far as all matters pertaining to the Peace Conference were concerned. He never once sought to appeal to his parliamentary majority to "support" him, when he was fighting to secure moderation at Paris. To do so would have been suicidal. Nicolson himself declares that "even as it was, there were moments when his [Lloyd George's] right to speak for Great Britain was slyly questioned: there were occasions when the statesmen of other countries endeavored to mobilize against him opposition elements at home, when they flirted both with the Tories, with the Left Liberals, and with the Labor recalcitrants; and throughout the period of the conference Lord Northcliffe, incensed at not having been appointed a Peace Delegate, turned upon Lloyd George a constant stream of boiling water." Well, the latter is the real opposition; a study of the newspapers of the period shows little evidence for the contention that other members of the Peace Conference tried to work with the Left Liberals and the Laborites, except where it was a question of the Americans trying to secure more moderation. No, the representative quality of Lloyd George for the purpose of making a sane and moderate peace was seriously impaired rather than improved by the election.

But how about the other argument, that Lloyd George could not have foreseen the outcome? Does a certain step cease to be a mistake because one did not foresee that one would stumble as a result of it? Does it become a regrettable necessity simply on that account? Other people in England, particularly the Left-wing Liberals and the Laborites whom Nicolson stigmatizes as recalcitrant (about what?), foresaw the outcome with laudable clairvoyance. Why could Lloyd George not have taken counsel with his former associates to whom in part he owed his political career? Clearly, there is no argument here.

Finally, it is urged, though not by Nicolson, that the election was overdue, because the life of Parliament had been artificially prolonged for the duration of the war. This argument was much stressed by Lloyd George in November, 1918, when he called the election. It is, and was, a weak argument indeed. Was the war really finished before the conclusion of the peace? Lloyd George might well have sought once more the liberal support of the majority which at the outbreak of hostilities dominated Parliament. There was much sane public opinion upon which to fall back, if a true statesman had wished to fight for a real peace on the basis of Wilsonian and of Liberal principles. No one can read the pages of the Manchester *Guardian* without coming to this conclusion. Consequently, Mr. Lloyd George and the imperialist Liberals whose mouthpiece he was cannot blame others for the foolhardy election by which they destroyed existing parliamentary and public support. Nor can they blame it upon circumstances; they are themselves responsible for it. It was a deliberate choice, by which they, politicians rather than statesmen, sought to secure another lease on power—and they got it.

The Rise of Popular Passion

The Khaki Election may well be called Exhibit 1, exemplifying the temporary outburst of reckless emotionalism in an electorate. Men counseling moderation and advising a just peace, like Mr. Ramsay MacDonald, were overwhelmed by rabble-rousers. Yet soon afterward, these same men were triumphantly returned to Parliament. It was too late. The treaties had been concluded, the damage done. It was not Lloyd George, of course, who pressed for a savage peace. In fact, he undoubtedly endeavored to stem the tide, to call back the spirits he had unloosed. But he was carried away by the current, in spite of better intentions.

In the beginning he was quite moderate: "We must not allow any sense of revenge, any spirit of greed, any grasping desire, to override the fundamental principle of righteousness." Perhaps it would have been more courageous to say "spirit of international conciliation," as the Manchester *Guardian* did, but even so the tone was moderate. But the hundreds of chauvinists beyond the Prime Minister's control began to rant almost immediately. The *Daily Mail* implored its subscribers to refuse support to any candidate who showed signs of "any tenderness for the Hun." There was little to restrain these jingoists, for the election was fought over no tangible issue. "What is it all about?" Liberal and Labor organs asked time and again in dismay and despair. Lloyd George, being the opportunist he was, had to drift with the winds which Lord Northcliffe and his ilk were stirring up; they created an issue for him. The outcome of this calamitous election became the conclusion of a vindictive peace. Nicolson admits that Mr. Lloyd George was affected by the jingoism of his "supporters." The conciliatory peace of Wilson's Fourteen Points had become a "relentlessly just peace." The Prime Minister, with the rest, clamored for Germany's paying the whole cost of the war, to the limit of her capacity.[3]

In short, this election, contrary to the older and sounder tradition of English parliamentary government, was a leaderless "consultation of the people." Mass opinion being what it is, the inevitable consequence was that the press magnates, rather than the people, had the final say. The electorate at large cannot speak, unless a clear issue is presented, and effective leadership endeavors to secure a particular answer. By calling the election of November/December, 1918, Lloyd George violated the spirit of English constitutionalism. He also showed how carefully it must be guarded, if catastrophes in international affairs are to be avoided.

The Election Which Never Was Held

What, then, should Lloyd George have done? It is rather easy to be wise after the event, yet it may serve a useful purpose here to consider the alternative course

[3] Nicolson seems to think that this phrase was a limitation. I believe that this is a case of reading later history into the facts. The emphasis on capacity which characterized the Dawes Plan had not been brought out in 1918. It was then a phrase emphasizing the *limit* rather than the *capacity*.

of action. Lloyd George, we make bold to assert, should have concluded his conciliatory peace, and then have called a general election in the summer of 1919 to secure popular approval of this peace. If he had done so, his figure would tower today as that of a great statesman. Democracy would have fared differently. The rasping echoes of the vindictive peace would not be resounding through Europe. This is said without any pretense at *ex-post-facto* prediction. Maybe he would have been defeated in that election; the men who were defeated in 1918 triumphantly returned to power a few years later. A new peace conference would have had to be held by those who defeated him. We are told that such delay would have been terrible. It is true. But have the consequences of the vindictive peace not proved more terrible? And then, maybe Lloyd George would not have been defeated. No one knows today what sort of peace would have resulted from genuine collaboration between true Liberals in England, America, and Germany. But I believe that Wilson, Rathenau, and a different English leader around the conference table could have routed the Tiger and his poisonous following.

Forgotten today is the wave of popular enthusiasm which greeted Wilson on his arrival in Europe. One can feel it, if one reads again the liberal and progressive papers. Generous sentiments were pulsing through France, England, and the rest of Europe. Superior British statesmanship might have been able at this crucial moment to bring to the fore in France a man like Aristide Briand. It certainly would have sought to negotiate a peace rather than dictate it. What peace such men might have made, we do not know; that it would have been a real peace, instead of a solemn mockery based on force, we may confidently assert.

What keeps alive our faith in the ultimate victory of democracy in foreign affairs is precisely this fact, that the international treaties which have thwarted its unfolding in the international sphere were made by men who rendered mere lip service to the democratic principles of international solidarity. By fighting for such a peace, first at Paris and then in Parliament and throughout England, Lloyd George would have saddled himself with a Herculean task. But democracy cannot live without leaders who possess the courage to bring out the forces for good which lie dormant in the people. He would have had to seek support first in Parliament among the majority which had dominated Parliament before the war. He would have had to play ball with Irish Nationalists, as he eventually did anyway. He would have had to seek a realignment with Asquith and the liberal groups further Left. A thorny path, indeed, but not a path beyond the capacity of a real statesman. When Bismarck was fighting with his king over the issue of a conciliatory peace with Austria in 1866, he threatened resignation if the king insisted upon humiliating the vanquished by having the Prussian army march into Vienna. His passion rose to such height that he kicked a table laden with precious crystal vases across the room, turned the mind of his king. To be sure, he was fighting for his ideal of a powerful national state; he wanted to secure himself against later Austrian revenge. But until the ideal of building international democracy finds statesmen of equally passionate determination, the forces opposed to it will triumph.

Summary and Conclusion

It has been argued in the foregoing pages that constitutional democracy is not as yet geared to the task of conducting foreign affairs. The people are of a divided mind; they desire both peace and the things which lead to war. What is more, they are politically divided on these issues. The conservative and nationalist parties emphasize the things which lead to war, the progressive and internationalist parties those aiding peace. A shift in control causes a democratic government to be wavering in its objectives. In seeking to strengthen the chances of peace through extending popular control, we have failed to consider these conflicting pressures. Education, while of some help, is less promising as an aid to democracy in international affairs than is often assumed.

Democratic theory and practice have failed to take account of the need for effective organization, though the makers of the American Constitution, as a notable exception, did so. The vindictive treaties at the end of the World War were a travesty of the genuine democratic impulse which had secured victory. The English general election strikingly illustrates the weakness of the democratic process. It should never have been called. The fact that it was called exemplifies the dangers resulting from having a politician rather than a statesman at the helm at a decisive moment. The course and outcome of the election unfold a vivid picture of the "gusts of popular passion" which the American founders so greatly dreaded. Had a conciliatory peace been concluded first, by genuine collaboration between Liberals in England and America, a very different general election might have been held later in an effort to secure popular support for it. The American Senate would have approached the problem of the League in a different state of mind.

But belief in the superiority of popular government need not be destroyed by these misfortunes. Indeed, it would have been extraordinary if democracy had at the first trial proved to be a smoothly working device in a field in which other forms of government never ceased to blunder. More patience is needed which would say, with Abraham Lincoln: "Why should there not be a patient confidence in the ultimate justice of the people? Is there any better or equal hope in the world?"

THREE

FOREIGN AND DOMESTIC AFFAIRS

The Threat to National Existence

THERE are frequent occasions when the issues of foreign and domestic affairs require conflicting solutions. Which shall prevail? Under popular government, the pressures exerted on behalf of a policy which is of immediate concern to some special group are apt to be much more insistent than the vague claims of national interest in the international sphere. Diplomats of the old school have always cited this fact as a decisive objection to popular influence in foreign affairs. Because international complications may threaten the very existence of a nation, it was held to be an unalterable principle that considerations of foreign policy should take precedence over those of domestic concern. What does this danger to the existence of the state mean?

Evidently, our thinking is cluttered up by reminiscences of the past. In the Greek and Roman world, with its small city-states built upon slavery, foreign policy did indeed affect the very existence of the state. Carthage and Corinth were completely destroyed. Others were reduced to lasting dependency.

During the age of monarchical absolutism similar catastrophes, like the partition of Poland and the absorption of Hanover by Prussia, stand as seemingly living proof of the verity of this principle. Failure to heed pressing international exigencies resulted in national disaster. At that time, the word "state" denoted the dynastic interests of a princely house and its political control over a given territory—a territory compounded of conquests. The failure of Poland to fall in line proved fatal.

During the nineteenth century, "state" acquired a broader meaning: the political organization of a united nation.[1] Once the state is thus closely related to the nation, we may well ask: What does a threat to the existence of the state mean? A complete destruction of such a national state is rarely, if ever, to be feared from similar states. Within the democratic context, the problem therefore reduces itself to a question of relative disadvantages; for who would doubt in this age of industrialism, of boom and depression, that mistakes in domestic policy may be as disastrous as those in foreign affairs? Is not the scourge of internal catastrophe to be feared as much as the terrors of war and defeat? And if so, might we discard the principle altogether? In such matters as immigration, trade and tariff, currency and money, foreign policy may suggest one course of action, domestic policy another. Perhaps a more refined pattern could be worked out to take the

[1] The extensive controversial literature on that subject is digested and to some extent noted in the article "State" in the *Encyclopedia of the Social Sciences*. See also F. M. Watkins, *The State as a Concept of Political Science*, 1934.

place of a mechanical application of the old principle, both in guiding and in interpreting action. But can foreign and domestic affairs be separated at all? Can a real distinction any longer be drawn between them?

Interaction Between Domestic and Foreign Concerns

While we all talk glibly of foreign policy as if it could readily be separated from the rest of national policy, actually the two are so closely connected that even a distinction in theory seems difficult to make. Take only the issue of prosperity. Governments the world over are struggling to plan their way out of depression. A common feature of all the plans has been rearmament on a large scale. These armament outlays have been accompanied by much blowing of the national defense trumpets. Bitterness and suspicion have been multiplied in the international sphere. Clearly the national interests at home and abroad are woven together into the same cloth. This close connection is no new thing. All through the nineteenth century, international economic relations continually expanded, trade and tariff treaties multiplied. Some optimists believed that an end to all war was being ushered in by this merging of national and international affairs. Even the rivalries seemed to make for solidarity. Prewar imperialism was presumably motivated by economic concerns. The need of domestic industries for raw materials and markets provided its most powerful stimulus. Anyone who has even glanced through the diplomatic documents available for the period will be impressed with how almost everyone took these needs of modern industrialism for granted. It may all have been a sorry delusion, as Langer argues.[2] For better or worse, delusions are just as powerful in motivating men as truths, if not more so. Certainly domestic concerns shaped foreign policy. Looking at the motivations behind policy, one can scarcely distinguish between foreign and domestic affairs.

The real distinction can be seen if we consider policy in terms of the obstacles placed in the way of its realization. Let us grant that there is only one national policy. Theoretically, it is compounded of what we, the people, would like to see done. Actually, such a national policy is never more than a hodgepodge of disjointed policies propagated and in turn opposed by various groups. But let us, for the sake of argument, assume for a moment that these internal struggles had been concluded, had resulted in the common acceptance of a truly national policy. Even then, such a policy would have to meet and overcome all kinds of obstacles. Laws, everyone knows, are more easily made than enforced. It is the distinguishing characteristic of what we call foreign policy that its most serious difficulties result from the action of other governments. In the old-fashioned language of Locke: "What is to be done in reference to foreigners depends much upon their actions, and the variation of [their] designs and interests." Hence, Locke thought that these matters "must be left in great part to the prudence of those who have this power committed to them." Evidently this father

2 William L. Langer, *The Diplomacy of Imperialism, 1890-1902,* 1935, ch. III.

of our constitutional lore believed that you could deal with foreign affairs as a distinct set of problems. It has been shown that this is no longer true. Almost every major issue of national policy has its "foreign," its international, aspect. If that be so, how can these international aspects be handled successfully? We may ask first of all: How have they been handled in recent times? Have these international aspects been given precedence or have they been confused with other issues?

The Effect of Democratic Conditions

An experienced student of French politics, M. Joseph-Barthélemy, contends that democratic states *should* ordinarily put considerations of foreign policy before internal issues, or, at any rate, *should not* allow internal issues to determine the course of foreign policy. For example, if additional armaments would trouble our international relations, we should not undertake them even if they might be beneficial in stemming a recession. Such rules are very well. They help our critical judgment. But what actually is being done? Exactly the opposite thing. Governments today allow internal issues to determine their policy, even when such a policy adversely affects the country's international affairs. They frequently do so in response to popular pressure.

Foreign policy is profoundly influenced by internal policy. Under popular government this is inevitable, since different parties hold different views as to what is in the "national interest." Such party controversies are very evident in certain phases of postwar politics, for example, the recognition of and policy toward the Soviet Union.[3] But it is not always clear whether these differences are the result of the parties' views concerning internal issues. When the German Communist party opposed Stresemann's Locarno policy, they may have been, as Stresemann charged, acting under instructions from Moscow. The Soviet Union was openly hostile to Germany's shift toward the Western capitalist powers. Yet they may also have been motivated by a desire to weaken Stresemann's "bourgeois" coalition in the *Reichstag*. Similarly, in the United States the opposition of the Republican party to recognition of the Soviet Union may be due as much to a fear that such a connection might strengthen radicalism in this country as to any doubts concerning the wisdom of such a step in foreign affairs.

An interesting illustration of the prevalence of domestic views, even without any clear conception of policy, is provided by our debt policy since the war. Many a senator who was publicly opposed to the cancellation of the war debts explained his attitude in private by the indifference or hostility of his electorate. He admitted that he had given up hope of getting voters to see the advantage of compromise, on this issue. Democracy here stood in the way of a far-sighted policy of international debt settlement, such as Castlereagh had pursued after the Napoleonic wars.[4] The internal issue of balancing the budget, of saving taxes,

3 See pp. 102 ff., below.
4 See E. F. Gay, in *Foreign Affairs*, IV, 394 ff.

loomed larger in the public's mind than any possible advantage in America's international position. This is a case of the people's preventing what might be a good policy. At other times the people may force a bad policy.

There remains, of course, the possibility of the government's disregarding the popular clamor. Such efforts tend to distort the policy at home. Under these conditions, the government, determined to pursue what seems the right foreign policy, soon finds itself without sufficient popular support. This was, in general, the fate of German republican governments. Their policy of fulfillment was sound, but highly unpopular.

Where democratic pressures are brought into play by special interest groups, highly compromising situations are apt to arise. A popular government may find itself forced into actions whose harmful effect abroad far outweighs the advantage gained at home. A good part of the high tariff policy falls under this head. Even more self-evident would be a case such as Japanese exclusion, brought about by pressures in California with most unhappy repercussions in America's relations with Japan. It will be necessary to examine each of these patterns in somewhat greater detail. For clearly, if democracy can only manage to live in splendid isolation, its prospects for the future are not very bright.

The People Force a Bad Policy

The blunders which were made at the Paris Peace Conference were to a considerable extent due to popular pressure, as we have shown in the preceding chapter. But internal issues played a minor role. True, the payment of reparations was wanted to make good the damages resulting from the war; but that was not an internal political issue in the strict sense. Striking cases of internal complications occurred in prewar England, for example. The English Liberal public was at the time bitterly opposed to any alignment with Russia. Left-wing Liberals and Socialists resented the suppression of their comrades under Czardom. Certain questions asked in the House of Commons at the time of the contemplated visit of the British fleet to Russia in 1906 will illustrate the point. These questions set the tone for attacks against the government on many later occasions.

On June 18, 1906, Mr. Thorne, a Laborite, said: "I beg to ask the Secretary of State for Foreign Affairs whether any representations will be made to the Russian government as to the treatment of officials of the people in the Russian Empire before the British fleet is sent on a visit of ceremony to Cronstadt and further steps are taken to commit His Majesty's government to definitely friendly arrangements with Russia." Sir Edward Grey replied: "The answer is in the negative." Mr. Thorne did not let the matter rest there. He soon asked again: "I beg to ask the Secretary of State for Foreign Affairs whether his attention has been called to the unchecked massacre of Jews at Bialostock now going on; whether he has observed the execution by hanging of children of tender age by the Russian government at Riga . . . and whether, seeing that this country broke off diplomatic relations with Servia, and is constantly remonstrating with Turkey for less serious outrages, he will consider whether the time has come that Great Britain should protest formally against the continuance of such practices, by the Russian government, and break off diplomatic relations until they are put an end to." Sir Edward replied: "The answer is in the negative." Finally, the matter took a more definite turn when Mr. Trevelyan suggested that the visit of the fleet might have a discouraging effect upon the Constitutionalist party in Russia, and Mr. Keir Hardie asked Grey in the House of Commons whether "he is aware that the Russian people are interpreting the meaning of the proposed visit of British warships to Russian ports to be that the British government sympathizes with the methods adopted by the Russian authorities for the suppression of the reform movement; and whether, under the circumstances, he will intervene to stop the visit from taking place." Grey replied that "if an impression exists in the minds of any section of the Russian people that the visit of the fleet is to be regarded as having any reference to internal affairs in Russia, it is quite incorrect. . . ."

These are far-off details, and it may be asked why they should be recalled, since similar remarks could be cited relating to more recent events. The reason is that we know the outcome of those controversies, and hence can draw the lesson. Did Sir Edward and the British government abandon the alignment with Russia? Not at all. Popular opposition merely drove the negotiations completely underground. Whether the policy of playing with Russia was a good or a bad one it is not necessary to determine. It is generally agreed that the secretiveness of the policy was very bad. A considerable body of opinion goes so far as to find here one of the major causes for the outbreak of the war. Open friendliness with Russia would have threatened the government's majority; to avoid the overthrow of the cabinet the policy was veiled.[5] The effect of bringing on the war was, of course, wholly unintentional. Still, there can be no doubt of the fact that parliamentary influence was a contributory factor.

Career diplomats, like Sir A. E. Crowe and Sir Arthur Nicolson, urged time and again that the existence of the agreements with Russia be made public. The agreements rested upon views accepted by all concerned. These diplomats felt, as did Grey, that there was a German menace. They all wanted to check this supposed "menace." But while Crowe and Nicolson believed that the best check lay in warning Germany of the isolation into which she was drifting, Grey, the leader in Parliament, was certain that the English public would not stand for an alignment with Russia and France against Germany. Hence Grey and his aides were confronted with the choice of doing one of two things, both of which they considered "bad foreign policy." One was to abandon the alignment with Russia and France against Germany, the other was to keep these agreements secret. They chose the latter. Both Poincaré and Sazonoff, the Russian Foreign Min-

[5] See Harold Temperley, "The Coming of the War," in *Foreign Affairs*, January, 1931, pp. 335 ff.

ister, have claimed that peace could have been maintained if the English cabinet had been frank about its relations with France and Russia. We shall never know whether this is true or not. It is clear that popular pressure was forcing what was believed to be a bad foreign policy.

For further illustrations, many cases of the postwar period could be adduced. But so much turns upon one's own view as to what constitutes a "good" or a "bad" foreign policy in these contemporary events, that it might be best to leave illustrations to the imagination of the reader. Most people in this country and in England would probably agree that the continuous nationalist pressure in France for a vindictive enforcement of the Treaty of Versailles represents one of the most consistently unfortunate instances of popular pressure in support of a bad foreign policy. But even this illustration may be argued about by some students of international affairs.

The People Prevent a Good Policy

The same difficulties in forming an objective judgment vitiate the discussion of cases where it may be said that the people, with their attention riveted on internal issues, prevent the adoption of a good policy. A clear case would arise only where, although it was generally agreed that a certain foreign policy was good, its adoption would be prevented by internal issues whose solution requires a different course. There are such instances, here and abroad. To pick one at random, let us take the Venezuela "incident" which occurred under Cleveland.

"A war-like gesture has been and may be employed in American politics to distract popular attention from economic crises and afford a covering for the suppression of discontents connected with crises. This fact is established and positively illustrated by the Venezuela 'incident' in the second administration of Grover Cleveland. At that time the country was suffering from severe economic distress. . . . At this juncture came the opportunity to arouse the multitude by a bold slash at Great Britain for an alleged effort to take territory in Venezuela. . . . Thereupon President Cleveland . . . made a threat of war against Great Britain, more open than veiled. He surely knew at the time that the diplomatic fulmination was calculated to ease the domestic conflict." [6]

The lesson is obvious. Let us take another case of more general significance. America's policy of aiding in the pacification of the world would be furthered a great deal if America could make generous concessions in the matter of tariffs. Yet such concessions are narrowly limited by what the various interest groups will stand. To be sure, the Roosevelt administration made some progress in this direction. Its good neighbor policy has crystallized into a series of reciprocal trade treaties. These may not have as wide popular support as some other phases of the administration's policies, but they are accepted by the public along with the rest. We can see here a great advantage which a

[6] Charles A. Beard, *Open Door At Home*, 1935, pp. 100-101.

presidential government, such as ours, has over a cabinet system dependent upon parliamentary confidence. No single policy can be picked out and made the ground for an overthrow of the government. The American government could recognize the Soviet Union without fear. It can enter into the negotiation of a trade treaty without having to worry that it might become the occasion for a general rout, as happened to the first Labor government in England in 1924. Ramsay MacDonald, it will be recalled, was defeated on the issue of the Soviet trade treaty.

But though a presidential government is more free to work out its own policy on special issues, it also is fettered. When dominant internal issues stand in the way it will hesitate to pursue policies generally recognized as good. Since the government does not possess the power to dissolve Congress and call for elections, it will be obliged to tread softly when the action of Congress is required. This is likely to be true wherever internal issues intrude themselves. The pusillanimous conduct of American foreign relations is generally believed to be due to this difficulty. Indeed, the United States government shows an inclination to soft-pedal all foreign policy because of such potential opposition.

All democracies suffer from the stifling effect of popular prejudice. The longing for isolation, for autarchy, is a deep-seated democratic instinct. Recently it has been in theory associated with the dictatorships. This is so, because the dictatorships are perverted democracies. They crave popular acclaim. Hence even the Hitlers respond to the isolationist sentiment which George Washington's Farewell Address so nobly voiced. But the dictatorial gesture is false, reactionary, oratorical. With the world becoming ever more closely knit together, this sentiment for living peaceably by one's self turns sour. It stands in the way of a desirable foreign policy capable of dealing with issues over which we have no control, and which we cannot get rid of as long as our industrial world endures.

The Government Persists in a Policy Which Is Considered "Bad" by the People

Let us now turn for a moment to what happens if the government fails to yield to popular pressures, and persists in policies which are popularly considered "bad." From a democratic viewpoint, such proceedings are hard to justify. They may bring on very serious crises. And yet, it may be necessary for the government to pursue such a policy. Democratic statesmen face their most heartrending tasks on those occasions when a certain foreign policy appears to them to be the only salvation for their country, and yet its adoption is opposed by a popular majority. They are then between Scylla and Charybdis, indeed. It is at such junctures that the arguments in favor of nonpopular government become almost unanswerable.

President Wilson probably was confronted by such a situation in 1917. He unquestionably had by that time become convinced of the necessity of America's entry into the war.[7] He probably convinced himself also that

[7] See Charles Seymour, *American Diplomacy During the World War,* 1934, particularly chs. I and V.

the people shared his views. Yet, Wilson has often been blamed for getting America into the war after having been elected on the slogan, "He kept us out of war." There are those who believe that a referendum taken at the time of America's entry would have shown the majority of the people opposed to that momentous step. Be that as it may, nobody will ever know. But we do know that Wilson learned the price a man has to pay for seeming to disregard the will of the people, when he was confronted afterwards by the sarcastic slogan, "Remember, he kept us out of war!"

A more recent instance is afforded by the English public's condemning the Hoare-Laval deal over Ethiopia. The Conservative party had recently returned to office on the promise of backing the League of Nations, sanctions against the aggressor, and respect for international law. Naturally Hoare found himself overwhelmed by general indignation when it became known that he had presumed to settle the Ethiopian troubles by conceding large parts of Ethiopia to Mussolini. It was necessary for him to resign from the direction of the Foreign Office. In the eyes of quite a few people, Hoare's action was later justified by the complete collapse and annihilation of Ethiopia, and he returned to office in a different, though scarcely less important, capacity. But that does not alter the evident conclusion that Hoare's endeavor to pursue his (perhaps intrinsically sound) foreign policy in the teeth of public opposition was a serious blunder.

If such tactics are persistently followed, they may have more baneful consequences than the overthrow of a single minister. The fate of the German republic was probably in large part brought on by the con-

(FITZPATRICK IN ST. LOUIS POST-DISPATCH)

Rome-Berlin Axis

tinuous pursuit of a foreign policy which remained unpopular with the masses. To be sure, skillful politicians like Rathenau, Stresemann, and Brüning were able to secure the necessary majorities in parliament. But mere majorities do not guarantee popular support, particularly when the majorities are very slight and require all sorts of compromises. For example, it is too often forgotten that the laws necessary for putting the Dawes Plan into effect were only got through the German parliament with great difficulty. In order to find the necessary two-thirds majority, Stresemann had to persuade the more conciliatory members of the Nationalist party under Professor Hoetzsch to bolt the party and vote for these laws. Punishment came to these men for their action: they were dubbed "yes men."

When in the early thirties it might have been desirable to take Hitler into the government, such a step was not taken for fear of its international repercussions. It is, of course, difficult to argue this point today when Hitlerism has wrecked German constitutionalism. But who can ever know whether a leader such as Brüning might not have succeeded in diverting the movement's destructive force, if Hitler had been made the member of a coalition government. Granting for a moment that such a thing might have been possible— and in 1931-32 many people believed it so—Brüning nevertheless remained resolutely opposed to taking the National Socialists into the government, unless they accepted certain conditions essential for keeping them in hand. Unless these conditions were fulfilled Brüning doubted whether the precarious state of Germany's foreign relations permitted such an experiment. He said so explicitly in a speech before the Executive Committee of his party.[8] Assuming that Brüning's states-manship might have transformed the National Social-ists into a responsible group while they had only 130 deputies in parliament, one might say that Germany's internal development was diverted by the necessity of giving primary consideration to her foreign policy. Within the democratic context, the old principle wreaked ruin upon those who followed its teaching.

The Triumph of Special Interests

Within the democratic pattern special pressure groups often are able to force their views upon admin-istrators and public alike. When this happens, the old principle is evidently placed in jeopardy. Such inter-ested pressures may cause serious difficulties, or they may remain rather innocuous in their effect upon the general course of foreign policy. It would be very wrong, however, to assume that their activity is lim-ited to democratic countries. They are and always have been active, and the only difference is that the work of such groups is more apt to come to the attention of the general public in a democracy. In his colorful por-trayal of the relations between Germany and the United States, Alfred Vagts has shown that special in-terest groups were just as actively at work in imperial Germany as in the United States, if not more so.[9] Im-perial Germany was, to be sure, on the way toward a measure of popular control, which, though it was nega-

[8] November 5, 1931. See *Frankfurter Zeitung,* next day.
[9] Alfred Vagts, *Deutschland und die Vereinigten Staaten in der Weltpolitik,* 1936, *passim.*

tive and limited in its scope, allowed such interest groups considerable influence. But even imperial Russia showed the impact of such special pressures. There is every reason to believe that special interest groups are also exceedingly active under contemporary dictatorship. Particular instances are hard to cite because of the secrecy of all proceedings. Yet there can be little doubt that hidden behind a screen of nationalist oratory these interests pursue their goals.

In a democracy, such group pressure need not be denounced, unless it takes surreptitious forms. A candid recognition of the many cleavages of interest and opinion which divide the public is the earmark of a working democracy. Unfortunately, the general public is so little interested in the international aspect of national policy that it is difficult to resist pressure from particular interests. The many kinds of indirect control which the United States has from time to time attempted in Central and South America fall largely under this head. They have been denounced as "dollar diplomacy." More recent efforts to substitute a co-operative pattern under the slogan of the "good neighbor policy" may be different in technique rather than in substance. The continued preoccupation of American foreign policy with South America may still be due to special interest pressures. The inherent importance of that sector of the world for the international position of the United States has not been increased.

Often such special pressures have given curious twists to national policy. Before the war, when France and Germany were certainly antagonists in the general theater of international affairs, the two countries co-operated in Turkey, particularly in the matter of railroad concessions. The financial interests of French and German investors were akin, and both were opposed to the English interests there. To take a different kind of pressure group, the anticlerical movement before and after 1900 forced the French government against its better judgment to abolish the embassy at the Vatican. Through this action the French control of Catholic missions in the Near East was endangered.[10]

In the postwar period, the co-operation of Germany, Hungary, and Canada in championing the rights of minorities before the League of Nations is curious and interesting. These national minorities, consisting of many millions of people of all sorts of nationalities, had organized themselves into an international body, the Congress of European National Minorities. This Congress had set itself up as a pressure group not only in the various capitals, but also in Geneva. Their rights having in part been acknowledged by the peace treaties, these groups soon commenced to complicate international relations between democracies in numerous ways. From the standpoint of democracy, their claims cannot be overlooked.[11]

[10] For details see Joseph-Barthélemy, *Démocratie et Politique Etrangère*, pp. 389 ff.

[11] This subject requires special treatment which the very extensive literature on national minorities does not cover. A careful critical bibliography down to 1927 is given by Jacob Robinson, *Das Minoritätenproblem und seine Litteratur*. An extensive discussion of the historical and legal aspects is contained in M. W. Royse's magistral treatise, *The Minorities Problem—The International Protection of Minorities* (forthcoming publication).

Various economic pressures have, of course, also been operative since the war. The role of the International Steel Cartel in furthering Franco-German *rapprochement* in the Stresemann era is well known, though the details are still a deep secret. The calamitous role which a lobbyist of American steel interests played at the Naval Disarmament Conference of 1927 was brought to light in 1931 by a Senate investigation endorsed by Herbert Hoover. Some interpreters go so far to attribute the rise of the Hitler movement to the financial contributions of the armament manufacturers. This thesis has in its favor that such interests have certainly derived enormous profits from the rearmament race going on all over the world. Whatever money they may have spent on Hitler was certainly well invested. But the entire rise of the movement cannot be attributed to these contributions. While some considerable sums undoubtedly went into the coffers of the party, their absence would not have prevented the movement.

The People's Voice as a Means of Diplomatic Pressure

Special pressures, as well as the pressure of the public at large, may be utilized by skillful diplomats for the gaining of national advantages. The German government might proceed to stir up trouble among the German minority in Lithuania, then protest against the maltreatment of the minority, and finally drop its protests in return for the tangible advantage of concessions in the commercial field. Such a charge was brought against Stresemann in connection with the negotiations over a commercial treaty with Lithuania. Similarly, the pressure of commercial groups will often be adduced by a government as the reason for their taking certain steps, though actually these groups could easily have been held in line if the government had wished it. The technique for playing up such special pressures is highly developed in France, where the press, especially the great Parisian press, is largely at the disposal of the government. Almost at a moment's notice, the government can set on foot a violent nationalist campaign in all the leading dailies. It can then point to these views as an insuperable obstacle to any concessions.

While such maneuvers have been perhaps more frequent in France, plenty of instances of such manipulation can be found elsewhere. Nobody who has studied the press conference as it works in the United States will question the possibility of its use for these purposes. The leading Washington correspondents are in and out of the State Department all the time. It may be enough to illustrate with a minor case which occurred a little while ago. Upon the return of the American ambassador, Alanson B. Houghton, a confidential press conference was held on March 17, 1926. This conference, though strictly confidential, was linked by the reporters with Mr. Houghton's reports to the President and Secretary of State. Acute disappointment was expressed over the League's failure to admit Germany. At the time, the Coolidge administration had incurred the wrath of extreme isolationists by accepting an invitation to collaborate with the

League's Preparatory Disarmament Commission. Hence the bad impression created by the League's failure to admit Germany probably caused the Coolidge administration to emphasize their disappointment in public. Indeed, it was said that the League's failure "had an intimate relationship to the proposed disarmament conference."

All this was quite contrary to the facts as we know them today. Houghton apparently felt at the time that fear of Germany's raising the disarmament issue had persuaded Britain and France that it was better to keep Germany out of the League. In this connection the newspaper reports spoke of Washington as skeptical of the good faith of European political leaders. They seemed ready, so the story ran, to betray the spirit of Locarno and to sidetrack disarmament. To complete the picture, the administration was represented as fearful "that there will be a new alignment of governments in Europe which will resolve the League into a series of the old balance-of-power groups." While there was recognition that the European outlook was bound to be different from America's, for geographical reasons, the fact remained "that nobody there is thinking seriously of disarmament." Later events proved this surmise to have been sadly accurate.

What is the lesson of this case? The American government used a "confidential" press conference to call forth the "pressures" it desired. In this effort it succeeded. Unhappily, the reporters' indiscreet linking of these facts with an ambassadorial report to the President caused a rather sharp reaction in Europe, particularly in France. There the implication that France was the villain in the piece pursuing a Machiavellian policy was keenly resented. In England, too, the imputation of bad faith caused bitterness. Consequently, the relations between the United States and England and France were adversely affected. What helped the American government at home, hurt it abroad.

The existence of such pressures has been so often alleged today for the mere sake of an argument that they are losing their importance. As usual, the dictatorships have gone the democracies one better in extending the abuse of democratic procedures. Hitler, as well as Stalin and Mussolini, turns to his mighty propaganda machines on the slightest provocation to unleash a "storm of indignation." Violent abuse is heaped upon the particular opponent at a moment's notice. It vanishes overnight if a shift in the diplomatic situation brings the wanted concessions or makes the dictator turn to another task. Hence, when such popular pressure is building up, people at once wonder how real it actually is. The people's voice as a means of diplomatic pressure is getting dim.

The Inadequacy of the Principle

All the foregoing shows that the principle of giving issues of foreign policy primary consideration is outmoded. It can no longer be considered a safe guide in modern diplomacy. This may not seem a startling conclusion to those who had quite forgotten that there ever was such a principle. But the power of ideas is such that they operate as strait jackets, and the more so, if one is not aware of their presence. Practically all contemporary diplomatic history is written *as if* foreign affairs were carried on in a vacuum, following their own laws and so clearly apart from the rest of national policy as to be capable of altogether separate treatment. From such thinking about what *has* happened it is quite natural to turn to discussing what *is* happening around one in that historical light. Indeed, it would be extraordinary if it were otherwise. In his brilliant analysis of the idea of national interest, Charles A. Beard has shown how the specter of an idea like that can haunt man's imagination.[12] It is very much the same with the notion of the paramount importance of foreign affairs.

The history of this country suggests that a nation may become a world power without making any real efforts in that direction. The recent history of Austria, on the contrary, shows that all efforts to remain a great power must fail, if the beckonings of democracy, of popular needs, and powerful group pressures are neglected. Karl Radek, in castigating the principle as an outworn bourgeois idea, claimed that "foreign policy is an outgrowth of domestic policy." This observation comes close to what must indeed be accepted for democracy. The course of foreign policy, "what is to be done in reference to the actions, designs and interests of foreigners," cannot be left "to the prudence of the governors," as traditional democratic theory

[12] See Charles A. Beard, *The Idea of National Interest,* 1935. An exposition of the close connection between domestic and foreign aspects in recent American policy is offered in ch. IX, "Foreign Implications of Domestic Affairs."

thought it could. If this were an ideal, static world in which all people were inclined to agree on a national policy, things would be easy. With the Communist who envisages such a world we could say that foreign policy was simply derived from domestic policy. But even the Communists have had their disagreements as to that "domestic" policy. Poor old Radek himself has been obliged to go down on his knees and stammer, "*Pater, peccavi,*" only to be condemned with the rest of those who thought Trotsky was right.

In democratic lands the formation of national policy is a continuous process, a free-for-all in which a multitude of interests and convictions get scrambled into an unrecognizable hodgepodge of partly contradictory policies. Foreign policy will dominate the decisions only to the extent to which the thought of the citizenry is concerned with foreign affairs. One view or another may dominate for a time. In his lucid analysis of the contrast between the industrialist and the agrarian policy, Charles Beard has erected symbols of such trends in the United States. He calls on us to cast these conglomerations of policy aside, and resolutely turn toward "The Open Door at Home." It is asking too much. Such unifying ideas may be reconstructed by the historian describing the past, though historians notoriously disagree. But that much consistency cannot be expected from a democracy. There are many voices for many visions.

Conclusion

The idea that the issues of foreign policy should take precedence over those of domestic concern was conceived in terms of ephemeral "states" rather than with regard to immortal nations. This conception is rooted in the conditions of an agrarian economy where national units are largely distinct from each other. All that is dead and gone. The rough-and-tumble of democratic politics has played havoc with the once-sacred principle of "high diplomacy." It has done so in sensible, unreflecting response to the actual life of our world.

But the maladjustments are numerous. Troublesome complications have arisen on every hand. The people, an infant giant, have been forcing bad policies, they have prevented good ones—good or bad, that is, not according to some abstract or ideal standard but according to the people's own ideas. Often the people have been asleep and special interests have triumphed in their name, twisting and diverting national policy until it became national catastrophe. Skillful manipulators of the game of politics, indifferent to the day of reckoning, have in turn utilized such pressures, in fact have set them afoot, to extort special concessions from their opponents in the international struggle.

To all this, there is but one answer: Democracy will march forward toward international organization. The same federative idea which in this country has merged sectional conflicts in a national pattern, however complex, will provide the framework for the slow evolution of a world policy. Separate national policy will become as limited in scope as state policy is in the United States today. But in the meantime democracies, while still wedged in between undemocratic systems, will have to pay for the permanent advantages of their freer life by temporary disadvantages and setbacks in the international game.

LIBRARY OF
Southern Methodist University
DALLAS, TEXAS

FOUR

CONTINUITY IN DEMOCRATIC FOREIGN POLICY

Democratic Policy Is Party Policy

FEW people fail to realize that in a working democracy, policy decisions are not made by the whole people acting in unison. The people are divided into parties, and these parties stand for and present alternative policies between which the people are asked to choose. Even this latter statement is somewhat remote from reality; for most of us are attached to a party and accept, over long periods of time, its policies without much argument. Yet, somehow, most people keep on talking as if parties did not exist in matters of foreign affairs. Even the brilliantly challenging pages of Charles A. Beard's *Open Door At Home,* with all their homespun realism, seem built upon the idea that general agreement is likely to prevail in regard to international relations. Perhaps this is a necessary approach for any man who wishes to appeal, to exhort, to lead toward a practical goal. But for descriptive or historical purposes we cannot avoid concluding that adoption of one kind of policy will call forth alternative responses from the other side, within a democratic framework. Unanimity is found only in heaven.

Democratic politics is party politics. Party politics operates by organizing the conflicting trends prevailing amongst the citizenry. Different ideas and opposing interests will associate themselves with the parties in the field, in the hope and expectation that victory will give them at least temporary ascendancy. This dynamic world of party politics introduces a measure of instability, of recurrent change and maladjustment into the relations of democratic states. Old-timers, like Bismarck, regarded this instability with deep distrust. Commenting upon the oscillations in policy between Disraeli and Gladstone, he remarked: "In England the basis of all political relations is more changeable than in any other state; it is the product of elections and the resulting majorities." [1] Bismarck could certainly have said the same about the United States. Here, such changes have become so much a matter of course that it is often not realized that their recurrent appearance violates another hoary principle of traditional diplomacy: the principle of continuity.

Of course, there are supposed to be certain guiding doctrines of American foreign policy—the Monroe Doctrine, for example—which are presumably not affected by changing administrations. But every student of American diplomacy knows that these supposedly fixed doctrines have undergone frequent modification.[2] Anyway, foreign policy is not compounded of doctrines, but of relations to other powers and their doings. Successive presidents are likely to have conflicting con-

[1] *The Kaiser vs. Bismarck* (ed. C. D. Hazen), N. Y., 1921, p. 173.
[2] See Benjamin H. Williams, *American Diplomacy—Policies and Practice* (1936), e.g., ch. IV.

ceptions of these relations, particularly if they belong to different parties. The names of Theodore Roosevelt, Wilson, Hoover, and Franklin D. Roosevelt epitomize such changes. Tangible and symbolic expression is given these changes by the automatic resignation of all ambassadors at the end of a president's term of office.

What is true of America is also true of Europe. The coming of democratic ways has subjected foreign policy to the pressure and exigency of party politics. But so deeply ingrained were the older ideas that this trend was resolutely resisted at first. Bismarck's scornful remarks about England in the seventies and eighties were founded on fact, but soon a reaction set in. Gladstone's Midlothian campaign of 1880, which injected issues of foreign policy into the election, aroused fierce resentment. At the time, Lord Salisbury wrote: "Under democratic control England must abandon all idea of influence upon the world's affairs; her statesmen must henceforth be content with a hand-to-mouth diplomacy which attempts no provision for the future." What occasioned so desperate an outburst? Gladstone had gone before the electorate with passionate criticisms of the English government's indifference toward the Bulgarian "atrocities" in Turkey. In doing so, he voiced the widespread indignation felt by the English Liberal public. As a result, he won a decisive electoral victory in 1880.[3]

---

[3] The apprehensions which such an event caused at the time can be seen in a letter Bismarck wrote in 1882 to the German Crown Prince: "The greatest difficulty in the way of giving *practical* expression to our relation with and inclination toward England lies in the fact that all confidential conversations are impossible because of the indiscretions of

The shock to traditional diplomacy was so great that after 1880 no effort was spared to protect its operation against popular outbursts. There is plenty of evidence to show that the continuity of British foreign policy was thereafter safeguarded in every way by responsible insiders. Indeed, so strong and immediate was the reaction that Gladstone himself could not effect any real change of policy in the Near East, such as he had advocated during the campaign. "A tradition of national policy independent of party changes was created, and the Foreign Office became as impenetrable and irresponsive as the Tomb." [4] Henceforth and down to the World War, English foreign policy remained largely removed from party politics. In spite of occasional protests in press and Parliament, the major parties did not make issues of foreign policy a significant part of their campaigns, and no essential breaks occurred as cabinets changed. It was only after the World War that foreign policy injected itself into party politics.

What was true of England was likewise true of France before the war. André Siegfried has roundly asserted that neither parliament nor the public was at

Cabinet Ministers toward Members of Parliament, and furthermore in the fact that no alliance can be secure because not the Crown, but one of the changing Cabinets would be responsible for it. It is difficult to initiate and to reach dependable understandings with England except in full publicity before all Europe. Such public negotiations exert in their first stages a bad effect upon almost all our other European relations, even when they come to nothing." See *Grosse Politik,* IV, 31/2, September 4, 1882.

[4] See Eugene P. Chase, "Parliamentary Control of Foreign Affairs," in *American Political Science Review,* XXV, 861 ff.

all interested in international affairs. That may be an overstatement. Certain it is that foreign policy was not an issue in election campaigns, and while it frequently provided the occasion for turning cabinets out, their successors furnished striking proof of the old adage, *Plus ça change, plus c'est la même chose.* From Freycinet down to the World War, French foreign policy remained unaffected by party controversy, or, to put it more exactly, party conflict over national policy largely neglected the international aspects of that policy. Such undemocratic continuity was pointed to with signal pride by Joseph-Barthélemy in rejecting the criticism of the foreign policy of the Third Republic frequently advanced by Royalist writers in France.[5] His argument is rather amusing. After having admitted that the great danger of a democracy is its instability, owing to the rapid change of cabinets and parties, he counters: "Obviously, France remains!" There exists, he believes, an incontestable reality, the national instinct. This instinct for the national interest made the Republic pursue the same policy that the kings had pursued of old.

"It was a matter of re-establishing through the constitution of symmetric groups of powers the equilibrium which had been broken by the attempted hegemony of Germany; what was needed was to satisfy the requirements of stability in international relations, and to guarantee peace through an equilibrium. This policy of peace through an equilibrium is the policy which has made France; it is the policy which during the most glorious periods of our history, the

---

[5] Joseph-Barthélemy, *Démocratie et Politique Etrangère* (1917), pp. 22 ff. and 62 ff.

immortal workers for our power and our unity have practiced, Henry IV, Richelieu, Mazarin. . . ."

But is this national interest really an infallible guide? The formula of the national interest puts the question of what is a desirable foreign policy, but it does not answer it. For what is in the national interest? Power, unity, peace—these are all so many weasel words. They do not tell us anything about the international aspects of national policy which we have to face at the present time, in France and England just as much as in the United States.

Ideas and Interests

"There are no ideas without interests, and no interests without ideas," declares Charles A. Beard and thus transcends both idealist and materialist approaches to history and diplomacy. Let us agree. Ideas totally devoid of interested support are dreams, or, in common American folk speech, ballyhoo. Interests without the ennobling support of ideas are lame, incapable of moving men beyond the interested circle. "National interest" is a useful term when you are engaged in pressing upon public attention your own view about foreign affairs. It may be doubted, however, whether, except in very general terms, such things as prosperity, security, and peace can be shown to mold policy.

These generalities are quite important. But there is little room for argument here, except concerning the order of their importance. Different foreign policies will emerge, if we urge one rather than the other of these three as our foremost goal. Yet, each advocate of a foreign policy will seek to make allowance for all of these things. Are they ideas or interests? Apparently, they are both. They are objectives.[6] As such, they have remained very much the same objectives they were in the days of monarchical diplomacy. But what has changed are the ideas as to how these objectives might be realized. We no longer believe, for example, that the hoarding of a maximum amount of gold will make us prosperous. We are beginning to doubt whether increased armaments will make us more secure.

While most of us are agreed on what we no longer believe, we are at odds about the alternatives. It is at this point that modern parties enter the picture. Knowing that ideas and interests go together, we can be pretty certain that the several alternatives are advocated by different interested parties. These "solutions" are not the same in all countries. Those rich in resources and geographically remote, like the United States, will find a different arrayal of interests from those poorly provided and exposed on all sides, like Germany. But traditionalism, Communism, and Fascism, as well as the milder variants of Socialism and imperialism, will have advocates everywhere. These ideas are all rooted in the problems which industrialism and nationalism, the two ogres of the modern world, have raised. Throughout the contemporary world, they are projected against the existing pattern of states which bring into the present their heritage from the past, a

[6] See Carl Joachim Friedrich, *Constitutional Government and Politics* (1937), ch. I.

distinct population, territories, resources, and so forth. Do these provide a permanent basis for foreign policy? Are the relations between nations molded into immutable patterns?

Factors Making for Continuity

The doctrine of continuity covers the most bewildering variety of policies. Some time ago, the Council on Foreign Relations, through its journal *Foreign Affairs,* sought to bring order out of chaos by persuading a group of prominent diplomats from different countries to write essays on the permanent bases of their country's foreign policy. These highly significant studies reveal the difficulty of discovering any such permanency.[7] Jules Cambon, in discussing French foreign policy, simply eliminates from consideration the aggressive designs of Richelieu, Louis XIV, and Napoleon as aberrations. He boldly asserts that France's cardinal aim has always been "security." In seeking to make good so startling a claim, Cambon exclaims: "Security! The term signifies more indeed than the maintenance of a people's homeland, or even of their territories beyond the seas. It also means the maintenance of the world's respect for them, the maintenance of their economic interests, everything, in a word, which goes to make up the grandeur, the life itself, of the nation."

If we turn to the German essay, we find an exact parallel to the French outlook. Herr von Kühlmann does not hesitate to reaffirm M. Cambon's plea. "Judg-

---

[7] The articles were subsequently published in the form of a book, entitled *The Foreign Policy of the Powers,* 1935.

ing by past experience, the goal of all German efforts in the domain of foreign policy must be security," von Kühlmann writes, adding that he considers Cambon's definition of security "masterly."

Unfortunately, if everything which "goes to make up the grandeur, the life itself, of the nation" constitutes "security," why then an insoluble conflict arises. On the one hand, we have Cambon's interpretation that 1871 "marked the end of that balance of power which under the leadership of France had guaranteed some sort of order in Europe." On the other hand Kühlmann reflects that "France has held to the principle that no unified Power must be allowed to grow up in Central Europe." He adds that "in accordance with this tradition she was bound to oppose by force the attempt to create a united and unified Germany."

Put into simpler language, the statements of these two distinguished diplomatists amount to saying that France and Germany must permanently fight each other, for the security of the one is the insecurity of the other. But are these permanent phases? Briand and Stresemann were, in their more hopeful moods, determined to bring these conflicts to an end. They did not succeed. Are we never to see another attempt? Many people in France and Germany would reject this kind of permanency. They would object to the continuity of such policies being in the national interest. Hence any argument concerning permanent policies which is thus rooted in traditions, which looks toward the past as inexorable precedent for the future, is deadening. Democracy cannot, will not, accept it.

Geographical Determinism

"The geographical position of a nation is the principal factor conditioning its foreign policy," writes Cambon. And von Kühlmann agrees by saying that "we are compelled to seek for light as to the permanent bases of Germany's foreign policy in her geographical position." This sort of geographical determinism is very popular in certain quarters at the present time. Indeed, a whole school has arisen, mostly in Germany, for whom all politics is determined by the material circumstances of geography: it is *Geopolitik*.[8] This view was first expounded upon a broad comparative basis by Friedrich Ratzel, who undertook to show that nations have grown from the soil, and that states are organisms. Such political Darwinism carries the fateful implication that the state must grow, if it is to live. Hence, international life is the life of the jungle. "The big fish devour the little fish by natural right," as Spinoza once wrote. The only obstacles to such growth are "natural, geographic" conditions. In slightly modified form, this grim view also dominates much modern history writing. That it has an element of truth can hardly be denied.

Yet, it is evident that geographical conditions become a deterministic fate only after we assume that growth is necessarily territorial expansion. Cambon

[8] See, for this group of writers, the learned study by Richard Hartshorne, "Recent Developments in Political Geography," in the *American Political Science Review*, XXIX, 785 ff. and 943 ff., 1935. Cf. also the recent article by Nicholas Spykman, "Geography and Foreign Policy," in the *American Political Science Review*, XXXII, 28 ff.

gives a beautiful illustration of how make-beliefs have to inject themselves before the geographical determinism will work, when he confesses: "The *belief* that the Rhine should be the national frontier has become a part of the national soul." Actually, then, it is rather a question of what Frenchmen *believe* when they think of their frontiers, or what Germans *imagine* to be the difficulties of their geography. Hans Grimm's enormously popular German novel, *Volk ohne Raum* (*Folk Without Space*), dramatized the agrarian land hunger, focused it so as to make territorial expansion appear absolutely vital to Germany's future. But Germany's density of population, while considerable, is not nearly so high as that of Belgium: to be exact, 363 to the square mile as contrasted with 705, as of 1933 and 1935 respectively. In view of all this, it is difficult to accept any kind of determinism.

Mountains, lakes, and rivers determine policy only after its objectives have been set by the will and imagination of the people concerned. If these objectives change, the mountains will not keep the policy intact. In ridiculing the idea of permanency in foreign policy, a leading Communist once commented that "it is silly to say that geography plays the part of fate, that it determines the foreign policy of a state. . . ." Still, geography remains a significant factor in the picture. Stalin, in explaining that the Soviet Union wants peace, observed that "the Soviet Union has everything necessary for the building up of a socialist society." Are we not entitled to infer that if the Soviet Union were not largely self-sufficient, then she might wage war to become so? It is, then, an exceptionally advantageous geographical position which makes the Soviet Union, like the United States, rather pacific.

There is one further consideration. Foreign policy, the international aspect of national policy, depends not only upon our own will, but upon the will of our neighbors, "the design of foreigners." Here geography cuts deeper as a fateful determinant. For a country with open frontiers is differently placed from an island, and a high mountain range may be as efficacious as a big army. Democracy tends to emphasize such permanent factors. Since they are material and readily observable, they stare people in the face, so to speak, and affect the thought of the man in the street very profoundly. It will always be much more difficult to put over disarmament with the German than with the American masses.

World Issues: International Socialism, Fascism, and Democracy

If democratic politics is party politics, it stands to reason that the course of national policy will become more unsteady as parties drift further apart. This instability is likely to have considerable repercussions in international relations. Indeed, the periods of great revolutionary upheavals in the world's history have always been accompanied by a pronounced lack of continuity in foreign policy. Even in the days of monarchical government this was so. In the sixteenth and seventeenth centuries, when religion was a mighty force in drawing states together, a shift or realignment of religious factions in a country was apt to bring on an international realignment. Thus, when Henry IV was murdered in 1610, the shock was felt throughout the chancelleries of Europe. His ardently Catholic widow, Maria de' Medici, was unwilling to carry out Henry's commitments to the German Protestants. More recently the French Revolution brought about many similar situations. In that period, it was a regular part of French diplomacy to seek the triumph of the ideals of liberty and equality abroad, and the relations between states were constantly changing as revolutionary groups won or lost. All international relations were affected by the shifting attitude toward the new ideas.

We have been witnessing the same problem all around us. British foreign policy, skillfully continued along traditional lines before the war, began to zigzag when confronted with the specter of Russian Communism. Intervention, nonrecognition, recognition, trade relations, actual alliance—they have all come within the compass of British policy during the two decades since the advent of Communism. The alternation between recognition and nonrecognition of the Soviet Union has been bound up with the shifts from Conservative to Labor governments. To the Tory policy of intervention, hostility, and nonrecognition, the Labor party opposed the policy of recognition, sympathetic co-operation, and even alliance. Labor may have felt ill at ease on account of the openly condescending attitude of Moscow. Naturally, they did not like to be dubbed "social patriots." But they had the courage of their convictions.

During the spring and summer of 1924 the Labor government negotiated with the Soviet Union a general treaty which was to settle all outstanding controversies between the two empires. After many difficulties such a treaty draft was finally agreed upon on August 10, 1924.[9] But there was general opposition to this treaty. The Conservatives, and even many Liberals, in Parliament and out, criticized the provisions of the draft. The agitation of the public became so great toward the end of September that a general election appeared inevitable. When the government suffered defeat in the House of Commons on October 8, Ramsay MacDonald carried the question to the people.

At that moment there appeared in the *Daily Mail* a letter which purported to have been written by Gregory Zinoviev, President of the Presidium of the Third (Communist) International. In this letter, Zinoviev gave instructions to the British Communist party as to how to conduct itself during the election, and how to carry on its work within the army for the purpose of "paralyzing all the military preparations of the bourgeoisie."[10] A parliamentary investigation later made it highly probable that the document was a fake. Things must have come to a serious pass when responsible politicians stooped to such tactics. Yet, the indignation which this letter aroused reveals the profound cleavage which divided the two major parties

[9] For this and the following see Louis Fischer, *The Soviets in World Affairs* (1930), pp. 471 ff., and William P. Maddox, *Foreign Relations in British Labour Politics* (1934), *passim,* for background.

[10] See for a full text Cmd. 2895 (1927), p. 30.

of Great Britain on this crucial issue of foreign policy. For it has been claimed that "the letter, when published, caused an unprecedented storm of excitement in England, and undoubtedly determined the outcome of the elections. The smashing victory of the Conservatives would have been impossible without it. Neither the Tories nor the Liberals nor Labor denied for one second the effect of the 'Zinoviev' letter in determining the constitution of the House of Commons from November, 1924, to June, 1929." Relations between Great Britain and the Soviet Union rapidly became strained until the final break occurred in 1927. As soon as Labor returned to power, in 1929, the policy was changed back again. These changes resulted in the most general discontinuity. For British policy toward the Soviet Union plays so central a role in British international relations as to affect all the rest, one way or another. It evidently influences Britain's relationship with Germany, Japan, Poland, the Little Entente, Turkey, and so forth. Discontinuity in this important policy has, therefore, made a large part of British postwar foreign policy vacillating and weak.

The agitation and uncertainty attending British-Soviet relations have more recently been paralleled by a similar controversy in France. Ever since the governments of the Left have entered upon a policy of collaboration with the Soviets, the internal situation has shown signs of considerable strain. This state of affairs is, at present, further complicated by another ideological force: Fascism. In spite of the deep roots which Republicanism has in France, this new set of ideas and make-believe is somewhat threatening in that country. Frenchmen usually deny the importance of the memories of Napoleon Bonaparte. But the cult of power is not unknown. Royalist opposition never quite died out under the Third Republic, but remained as an intellectual fad. Henry Lichtenberger has put the matter well: "Certain groups oriented to the Right . . . have been seized with tenderness for the dictatorship established across the Rhine by Hitler. The movement toward the Left in France has profoundly disturbed these groups, has threatened their sense of security even more than Hitler's Germany. These circles have been watching with deep distrust Léon Blum's policy of a rapprochement with Soviet Russia, and of giving aid and comfort to the Spanish Loyalists." Describing the French attitude, Lichtenberger observes: "We float about amidst thousands of conflicting sentiments ranging from decided horror through mistrust and uneasiness up to curiosity mixed with sympathy and regret that we do not have a 'strong man' like Hitler in France."[11] It goes without saying that such a state of public sentiment exposes foreign policy "to the gusts of popular passion," in Alexander Hamilton's quaint phrase. Continuity of foreign policy under such conditions is unlikely indeed.

The League as an Issue of Party Politics

Besides the great revolutionary challenges of Communism and Fascism, the League of Nations must not

[11] See Henry Lichtenberger (transl. K. Pinson), *The Third Reich* (1937), p. 281.

be forgotten. Much thought has been given to its role in international life. It is sometimes forgotten how much it has also injected itself into domestic politics. Perhaps the most startling indirect effect of the League, undreamed of by its creators in 1919, is the leaven which it has proved to be in stimulating partisanship concerning international affairs. In practically every European country public opinion and parties are distinctly divided on this issue. Not that it necessarily takes the form of thoroughgoing opposition. But conservative and nationalist elements distrust the League as an instrument of diplomacy, render it mere lip service, and interpret its sphere as narrowly as possible. Progressive elements are inclined to take the opposite view.

When the Labor party took office in England in 1924, that shift soon was followed by a similar one in France, where Herriot and his Leftist Coalition (*Cartel des Gauches*) supplanted Poincaré in May, 1924, bringing Aristide Briand back into power. As a result, these progressive leaders on both sides of the Channel at once initiated a program for strengthening the League as an instrument of international diplomacy. The upshot of these efforts was the so-called Geneva Protocol. The central purpose of this agreement was to put teeth into the international sanction machinery under the League.[12] Its initiation was undertaken in an atmosphere of profound enthusiasm at Geneva—one of the

---

[12] J. P. Baker, *The Geneva Protocol,* London, 1925, and D. H. Miller, *The Geneva Protocol,* New York, 1925. The Protocol was unanimously "welcomed" by the delegates of forty-eight states at Geneva, on October 2, 1924.

high-water marks of internationalism after the war. At that time (September 6, 1924) Ramsay MacDonald said in the Assembly:

"Sir, if this meeting of the Assembly could only be recorded in the pages of history as the Assembly which, for the first time, gave not only lip-service, but brain-service, it would be distinguished above all the assemblies of mankind that have met hitherto.

"My friend, M. Herriot, delivered an admirable speech yesterday. M. Herriot and I very often start on the same road, on the same journey, he on one side of the road and I on the other. The road is the same, the end is the same, and as we are good friends we do not go very far before we move together and continue our journey arm in arm in the middle of the road. It is not that our opinions have been reconciled; it is that the meaningless difference in distance and in position has been bridged by our common sense and our desire for human companionship. . . ."

To this outburst of friendly feeling Herriot responded:

"We both arrived here only a few days ago with a deep sense of our responsibilities and a keen anxiety to know whether we could be useful or not to the great cause of peace. . . . We have both spoken freely. We have explained our ideas, our fears, our methods. . . . The road of which my friend MacDonald spoke just now is still a long road, but we shall advance along it, he and I, together, arm in arm, at one in our thoughts and in our efforts." [13]

This sort of outright internationalism was discontinued as soon as the Conservatives came into power. Austen Chamberlain, of Locarno fame, declared on the

[13] League of Nations, *O. J. Records,* 5. Assembly, Geneva 1924, p. 78.

cabinet's behalf in the fall of 1924 that they did not favor the Protocol, that the time had not yet come for such international action; the Conservatives preferred regional agreements. The British ambassador in Berlin, Lord d'Abernon, himself a Conservative and a friend of Curzon, soon afterwards began the historic conversations with Schubert and Stresemann which led to Locarno and to Germany's entry into the League. The Conservatives were not opposed outright to the League, but they wished to have its sphere of action strictly defined. Such ideas as those contained in the Protocol might become troublesome to the Empire.

Perhaps no country in this period illustrates more strikingly than Germany the curious way in which the League was tied up with party politics. At first, Stresemann's policy of seeking Germany's admission to the League was much criticized in nationalist circles, even in his own party. But gradually, as Stresemann's Locarno policy won a measure of popular approval, and as it became apparent that Germany's antagonists, internationally, such as Poland, were trying to interfere with Germany's entry, nationalist opinion grew more favorable. Indeed, when the entry could not be effected in the special session of March, 1926, many German nationalists, instead of rejoicing, bitterly complained about this "defeat." However, their support of Germany's being in the League was not long-lived. As they soon discovered that Germany's position was not too comfortable, and that Germany's delegates often returned from Geneva without very substantial gains, they began to rant. Agitation became more violent when the League proved itself severely handicapped in making progress in the matter of disarmament. Soon popular clamor demanded that Germany must quit the League in order to maintain her self-respect. Particularly in the agitation of Hitler, this demand was featured prominently. No step was more predictable than that Germany would leave the League when he came into power.

As everyone knows, Germany's and Japan's withdrawal from the League brought the Soviet Union into it. This was a complete reversal of the trend of international alignments prevailing from 1919 to 1933. There had been more than a grain of truth in the oft-repeated accusation of Moscow that the League was organized as an *Internationale* of the capitalist powers to combat world Communism. Everyone who has read the negotiations leading to the adoption of the Covenant will admit that it was out of the question for the Soviet Union to be a member of the League. Membership would have seemed a solemn mockery on the day after the Allied interventions in Russia. Nor can there be any question that in countries like France and Switzerland, where dominant popular sentiment is opposed to the Soviets, this membership of Russia has greatly weakened the League. The League has, in fact, become in the minds of many conservative Frenchmen almost as objectionable as Moscow. Leftist support of the League, on the other hand, has remained quite ardent. For these progressive groups the League and its defense are essential parts of any foreign policy they would support. Evidently, the League is another link between international and party politics. Irrespective of what little power it possesses, Geneva has become today a symbol of a hopeful approach to international affairs in many European countries.

The Constant Shift of Alignments

The story of international diplomacy since the war resembles the famous French soup, *bouillabaisse*. It is truly a medley of oddly assorted fish. As cabinets came and went in England, France, and Germany, not to speak of the smaller countries, one could observe a continuous shift of alignments. Indeed, there appears to be a curious rhythm of coming and going in the major countries. Unfortunately, such coincidences as the simultaneous appearance of a progressive government in both England and France in 1924 remained an exception. Indeed, between France and Germany there is discoverable rather a hapless tendency for the two countries to move in opposite directions. Thus when a conciliatory Progressive coalition would be coming into power in one, a nationalist Right-wing group would make its appearance in the other. This was the situation immediately after the war; it remained essentially the same paradox throughout the postwar period. When in 1924 Herriot and Briand came into power in France as a reaction against the Ruhr policy of Poincaré, a Rightist coalition under Luther was emerging in Germany. When that coalition had worn thin in 1926, and the pendulum was swinging Left in Germany, Poincaré was back in power in France. When Germany at last succeeded in digesting the full meaning of Stresemann's policies, and returned a Left majority, in the spring of 1928, a Right reaction had set in in France carrying Tardieu into power. Once more a statesman with an international vision appeared in Germany, in the person of Brüning. When his policies promised to come to fruition, with a return to the Left in France in the spring of 1932, Brüning was overthrown by a Right reaction which carried Germany forward into the nationalist extreme of Hitler. It was as if some evil genius sought to insure that internationally progressive governments should not be in power at the same time in both countries.

These criss-cross changes, necessitating a constant readjustment of international relationships in all directions, suggest that a more stable organization of democracy than that characteristic of France and Germany under their curious multiple-party parliamentarism might be of considerable help. However, a toning down of the democratic impact would merely delay, but not fundamentally change, the workings of this international system.

It is rather interesting that during this period efforts were actually made to manipulate internal party reactions in the interest of international agreements. In connection with some ticklish questions at Locarno, Stresemann noted down such a plan. "Briand appeared willing to make an agreement for announcing certain changes in a parliamentary speech after getting in touch with us [the Germans] concerning this speech. Perhaps it would be well to set the same day for the parliamentary debate in both countries."[14] A similar technique was suggested again a couple of days later. It clearly shows the need for international co-operation on the party level.

The United States in World Affairs—a Stable Course?

Compared to this complicated pattern of constant changes and realignments, the United States seems to have pursued a much more stable policy. Under its presidential form of government, changes are much less frequent. Moreover, the long periods of predominance by one party and then another further tend to stabilize foreign relations. Of course there exists, in the United States, Congress's very immediate concern with foreign affairs, because of the Senate's special powers in that field. Recent investigations have shown, however, that the Senate has taken a much less active part in foreign affairs than was commonly supposed.[15] On the whole, it has uniformly been inclined toward a greater measure of isolation than the executive branch. It voted down the League, though with a very narrow margin, and it has time and again defeated the World Court. But on the whole the country's foreign policy has been fairly continuous during the Republican tenure, 1921-33, and then again during Roosevelt's two terms. The important new approach to international affairs on the American continent, symbolized by the "good neighbor" slogan, has meant a restriction of the Monroe Doctrine, and a continuous effort to-

---

[14] *Gustav Stresemann, Vermächtnis,* II, 195.
[15] Royden J. Dangerfield, *In Defense of the Senate,* 1933.

ward opening up new trade by specific agreements. Perhaps the most noteworthy departure was the recognition of the Soviet Union in 1934.

By comparison, America's foreign policy has been a model of stability. This is, of course, usually attributed to the country's isolationist tradition, to its remoteness from theaters of conflict. But it would seem that our constitutional arrangements help in bringing about this happy result. National elections which come along every four years, and not necessarily at times of popular excitement over some issue of international affairs, are likely to be fought over national policies in terms of their domestic rather than their international aspect. Certainly in the re-election of Roosevelt, international affairs were not crucial. A study of the slogans of presidential campaigns reveals that only a few have been focused on issues of foreign affairs, for example, the second Wilson campaign. In most of them, these matters play a minor role. But there can be little question that these dormant issues may be awakened, and the inherent rule of democracy prevails here as elsewhere—that there can be no continuity, unless the electorate acquiesces in the policies which are being pursued.

Conclusion

From the foregoing discussion, the conclusion is suggested that democratic foreign policy is the more continuous the less active it is and the less interest the citizenry takes in it. Hence, in terms of democratic principles, continuity cannot be looked upon as a good thing in itself. The mocking remark that continuity is a virtue only when the policy to be continued is good calls attention to the essentially fragmentary and controversial nature of all policy. From a democratic standpoint, there is no obviously "good" policy. Once the community has taken a real interest in foreign affairs, it is bound to develop different views about what is a good policy.

From the standpoint of the student of international affairs under democratic conditions, the decisive lesson is this: never to interpret democratic foreign policy merely by states, but always politically and with reference to parties and groups. In other words, it is not simply France or England which must be looked upon as doing this or that, but rather progressives or conservatives, or what not, in England or France.

Bismarck's objections to the ever-changing cabinets in England were perfectly natural. He was engaged in the secret machinations of *Machtpolitik* which it was difficult to carry through in England then. A democratic statesman would not raise such objections; he would not seek any alignments except in keeping with a party program, the general outlines of which are known to the public anyway. There will still be a measure of secrecy, but it will be limited to the initiating of negotiations—and it can never prevail for any length of time, except as a result of public indifference. Public indifference is a very real factor in democratic countries. Professor G. G. Wilson loves to tell a tale illustrating such democratic "secrecy." He had, in a meeting, mentioned some features of American diplomatic negotiations which were not generally known, and so caused quite a little newspaper comment. Soon he received a protest from a friend in the State Department who expressed amazement that Professor Wilson, of all men, should have been indiscreet in making public so important a secret. To his friend's indignant letter, Professor Wilson was able to reply: "Dear Friend, I am not at all surprised that you should be thinking ill of my revealing these facts. For they are only to be found in the most secret of all places, the Congressional Record. . . ."

Discontinuity is inherent in the democratic process in so far as policy is tied up with the party struggle. But there are broad policies common to all democracies and common to all parties: the principles and procedures of democracy itself. These require the extension of the idea of community and good fellowship to the relations with other nations.[16]

[16] See for a more extended discussion of the American position the statesmanlike address by Secretary of State Cordell Hull, printed in the Appendix.

FIVE

THE BALANCE OF POWER VERSUS THE LEAGUE

The League Ideal

THE many failures and defeats which have been suffered by the League of Nations in recent times have destroyed the vision which animated its builders. Still the difficulty of attaining an ideal is no conclusive argument against it. Certainly democracy is as yet an unfulfilled dream, a grand design which many a generation will have to struggle to develop and adapt to its problems and needs. It shows a curious impatience to expect success within the short space of a single generation for an ideal which transcends the rooted habits and prejudices of centuries. The present weakness of the ideal is due to its inadequacy. No ideal is a static picture on the wall. Plato could envisage his ideas as such immutable patterns of eternal verity. Western man conceives his ideals as projections of human aspiration. Hence they are molded, changed by the experience of the idealist. In 1919 the League of Nations was conceived as a world-wide organization including all states of whatever nature. Its machinery was supposed to bring to an end the "old and now forever discredited game of the balance of power." But the League ideal, so conceived, turned out to be unrelated to essential experience. It was found that the organization was not world wide, but limited in membership. The very people whose president had voiced the early aspiration turned against the attempted realization. Were the Americans entirely wrong? Were their objections unexplainable, except in terms of prejudice and narrow interest? Or was their reaction also influenced by a feeling, no matter how vaguely expressed, that the League ideal was wrongly conceived, that there was something essential missing which their democratic experience demanded?

The American Constitution provides in its Article IV, Section 4: "The United States shall guarantee to every State in this Union a Republican Form of Government, and shall protect each of them against Invasion; and on Application of the Legislature, or of the Executive (when the Legislature cannot be convened) against domestic Violence." This provision, closely paralleling similar ones in other constitutions, expresses the need for a certain measure of homogeneity in every federation. Immanuel Kant, in his celebrated *Essay Concerning Eternal Peace,* confirmed the teachings of experience by the logic of theory. In the first article of his projected pact to establish eternal peace, he insisted that every member state must have a republican constitution. What is more, he defined the republican constitution in terms of the American conception as liberty and equality of the citizens under the law. Kant felt that only this kind of government is suitable to collaborate in an international organization, because only here the citizens take an active part in determining foreign policy. The Covenant of the League of Nations originally recognized these teachings of experience and philosophy. It provided for membership of the "free governments." But soon the exigencies of practical politics interfered. Governments which were anything but free were accepted as members. Many of the League's most humiliating experiences are the result. Instead of terminating the membership of Germany, Italy, or Japan, when these countries ceased to possess constitutional democratic governments, the League awaited, tremblingly, the moment when such a state would with loud-mouthed oratory declare its withdrawal of membership. There was a serious weakness in the early ideal. The institutions derived from the ideal suffered from this defect. Born of the enthusiasm for "the irresistible progress of democracy," the actual League may perish, unless it is rebuilt to conform to a sounder ideal. The new organization could, at the same time, be removed from all connection with the interested desire to buttress special and temporary provisions by international sanctions.

The Balance of Power Ideal

When the ideal of the League of Nations was crystallizing, twenty years ago, it was natural to contrast it with what appeared to be the reality of the balance of power. The latter seemed an irresponsible, if not a vicious, game, indulged in for the sake of aggrandizement by the old secret diplomacy. It was natural to draw this contrast, but it was not wise. For the balance of power also had its ideal conception. Curiously enough, it, too, was conceived of as an instrument for maintaining peace. Indeed, incredible as it may seem today, the theorists of the balance in the seventeenth and eighteenth centuries saw in it a "beautiful design." At that period, men were seeing "natural balances" everywhere. There was Galileo's and Kepler's balance of heavenly bodies in the universe, followed by Selden's balance of trade and by Harrington's and Locke's balance of power within the state, and finally Shaftesbury's balance of affections.[1] The fundamental basis for these conceptions of a balanced existence lay in the firm belief in the "pre-established harmony" of the universe and a similar natural harmony of interests in society. Its latest and most potent expression appeared in the economics of Adam Smith and the classical school. According to them a harmonious society would result if each person pursued his own interests.

We have come a long way from such notions. The belief in a natural order is fast disappearing, though there are still remnants here and there, such as the large group of conservative individualists who would have us return to laissez-faire in the economic realm. Even such persons do not often believe in the balance of power in international affairs. As an ideal it is gone. Yet, how was the ideal ever envisaged? How could a balance of power maintain peace? Like all ideals for

---

[1] See Karl Pribram, "Die Idee des Gleichgewichts in der älteren nationalökonomischen Theorie," in *Zeitschrift für Volkswirtschaft* (1908), XVII, 1 ff.

action it was supposed to be derived from experience. What was this experience? Let us illustrate by a simple case.

Suppose there were only three countries in the world, fairly alike in power and resources. Country A, being a bit stronger than C, may be tempted to make war

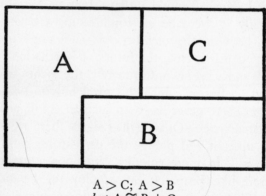

$$A > C; A > B$$
$$\textit{but } A \cong B + C$$

upon C. If it could conquer C, it would then be strong enough to overpower B and establish world dominion. Hence, it would appear as the better part of wisdom for B to suggest to A that it would not suffer such an attack upon C, and thus maintain the existing balance of power. In short, thus simply conceived, the idea of a balance checks the aggrandizement of one country at the expense of others, and maintains things as they are. If the idea would work perfectly, there could never be a war. Stated in such simple terms it is, indeed, a beautiful design.

Orthodox international law has not hesitated to make

this ideal conception the foundation for its normative structure. It assigns to the balance of power a central place in its system. We are told that "an equilibrium between the members of the Family of Nations is an indispensable condition of the very existence of International Law." Lest we forget, we learn also that "the first and principal moral is that a Law of Nations can exist only if there be an equilibrium, a balance of power, between the members of the Family of Nations." [2] If this is true, the future of international law is black indeed. For, unfortunately, the reality is complicated by factors which this ideal fails to take into account. There never has been such an equilibrium as an isolated system. Outside the balance there are forces which upset it and plunge the participants into war. Worse still, in more complex situations a master of statecraft like Bismarck can employ the balance of power for the purpose of maintaining peace everywhere, except at the point where he wishes to strike. Has not Japan's game been the same in the last couple of years? A complex balance of Germany against France and Russia, Britain against Islam and Italy, leaving the Empire of the Rising Sun a free hand in Asia? Should we not perhaps even interpret Britain's old tradition in those terms: peace in Europe in order to enable her to concentrate her power on her empire overseas?

2 See L. Oppenheim, *International Law* (1928), I, 99 and 268. To argue, as does Charles Dupuis, *L'équilibre Européen* (1909), pp. 98-99, that the balance of power is not a *principe de droit,* because it lacks clarity and specific content, is correct. But such an argument does not meet the notion that the balance underlies international law as its only effective sanction.

Historical Sketch of the Reality

Tied up as the balance of power game is with international rivalry of any sort, it is self-evident that its practice goes back to the dawn of history. This is now generally acknowledged. "The balance of power as a pattern of political relationships is clearly apparent in the early city-state systems of the Tigris-Euphrates valley and in the relations of the great oriental monarchies of the ancient Near East. It likewise appears very distinctly in the international politics of the Greek city-states and also emerges in the larger State System of the whole Mediterranean basin during the second and third centuries B.C." [3] But from these balances, existing as a matter of fact, we must distinguish the rise of the idea as an ideal. For this idealization of reality in terms of ethical purposes is a peculiarity of our Christian civilization. Evidently, the balance of powers as an ideal had no place in the thought of men as long as a universal empire and a universal church were commonly believed-in forms of organization for mankind.

The protracted struggle between empire and papacy, continued between the papacy and the rising national kings, gradually destroyed the belief in universal rule. Indeed, by the fifteenth century, the relations between the papacy and the other Italian states showed all the traits of the balance of power practice. Hence, we cannot be surprised that the balance of power as an idea and an ideal makes its appearance in the histories of

[3] Frederick L. Schuman, *International Politics* (1933), p. 55.

Florence at the time of the Medici around 1500. Bernardo Rucellai (1449-1514), brother-in-law of Lorenzo de' Medici, is usually credited with having given the first explicit statement of the idea. He, as well as Guicciardini, both partisans of the Medici, have given wide currency to the notion that Lorenzo de' Medici was the inventor of the idea of such an equilibrium; in collaboration with Ferdinand of Naples he is said to have achieved a state of lasting peace.[4] But one wonders whether the idea did not originate with the papal diplomacy. Other things being equal, the idea has always had a peculiar appeal to powers lacking in military strength. The papal claims to being a universal umpire, to being *arbiter mundi,* if not *imperator mundi,* suggested as desirable a balancing of secular powers. In order to escape from the disorder of a multiple state system, the doctrine of a natural balance of such divided power might serve. The Church would undertake to maintain the balance, as a neutral arbiter supported by divine guidance. The idea of a balance of power seemed to reduce power's demoniacal force to calculably manageable proportions. To men increasingly imbued with the commercial spirit, with the desire to count and to calculate, such an idea had undoubtedly great attraction. It was the spirit which in our day is dubbed the spirit of capitalism, which is here seen to pervade the political sphere.

The concept appears again, and in a distinctly secular

---

[4] This view is maintained by Ernst Kaeber, *Die Idee des europäischen Gleichgewichts* (1906), pp. 12-13, where Rucellai and Guicciardini are accepted at their face value.

garb, in the course of the sixteenth century. It became
the battle cry of those who were pitted against the imperialist aspirations of the Hapsburgs, particularly
Charles V. Universal dominion, linked with the ideals
of peace and religious unity, is at the core of the imperial concept of Charles.[5] Charles's was a last titanic
effort to revive and pit the medieval universalism
against the rising tide of the modern Leviathan. He
was the Don Quixote on the imperial throne. Francis
I of France time and again invoked the ideal of an
international balance of power against this imperial
dream. Venice, and Henry VIII, the papacy and the
Protestant princes of Germany—all were urged to support Francis in his struggle. And though the vision of
Charles died with his abdication, the policy of Francis
was continued by his successors, as long as the Hapsburgs continued to hold a predominant position. Even
Richelieu drew extensively upon the doctrine in his
negotiations with England, Holland, and other states,
as did the Dutch leaders of independence before him
in their long protracted wars against Spain.

After the ravages of the Thirty Years' War had reduced the Austrian Hapsburgs, and after Spain had
been disintegrating from within, the policy Richelieu
had initiated gave France a predominant position in
Europe. Soon the imperialist aggression of the Sun
King, Louis XIV, brought all Europe together in a
mighty alliance, in the construction of which England
played a considerable role. This coalition was, however, an alliance for war, and thus does not fit into the

⁵ Peter Rassow, *Die Kaiseridee Karls V*. (1932), *passim*.

balance of power ideal. It was only after its victories and the peace of Utrecht (1713) that the balance was re-established. A similar situation arose a century later, after Napoleon I's armies had swept over Europe, subduing one country after another. Once more the threat of universal empire appeared. A coalition to put him down was formed and defeated him. Afterwards the Congress of Vienna, conceived in terms of a new balance of power, established the European Concert which left England as the *arbiter mundi*.[6] Castlereagh and Canning labored diligently to maintain the complexly balanced equilibrium which had been established at Vienna. Great Britain, concentrating her energies on the Empire, avoided territorial acquisitions on the European continent. Hence she was able to maintain her ascendancy for nearly two generations. Both France and Russia made intermittent efforts to displace her. They did not succeed, though Napoleon III flattered himself that he had.

A serious challenge came with the rise of the Bismarckian Empire. By a series of skillfully prepared wars against isolated neighbors, Bismarck succeeded in becoming the arbiter of Europe's quarrels, while England withdrew into splendid isolation. But Bismarck's was an unstable and purely personal dominion which petered out with his fall from power (1890). There was no one to resume the role of Castlereagh or even Palmerston in England. After some overtures to Germany which were blindly rejected by subaltern

---

[6] C. K. Webster, *The Congress of Vienna 1814-1815* (1919). See also his *Canning*.

intriguers,[7] Britain allowed herself to be tied into the Franco-Russian combine which had sought to balance the Triple Alliance of Germany, Austria-Hungary, and Italy. But was this really a balance of power, as Wilsonian idealism assumed? Certainly, it was not in keeping with the ideal; for it brought on the war. But had not other balances done the same and simply proved once more that the ideal of an equilibrium of power was a pipe dream?

The Balancer

It is our contention that something quite essential was lacking in the picture of the decade before 1914. The little thumbnail sketch of diplomatic history as it relates to the idea of a balance of power revealed that there has been a *balancer* behind each balance. The power equilibrium has never worked when it was merely looked upon as a dead, material equipoise of forces. From the very beginning, when the Florentine historians wished to flatter Lorenzo il Magnifico, the idea has always been linked with an active scheme of some government. Such a government expects to be the "laughing third" party in the situation, deriving power from its being the arbiter between the powers in the balance. In the great struggle between Francis I and Charles V, England for the first time stepped forward to assume this papal role. It was then that Henry VIII proudly stated: *"Cui adhaereo praeest."* The fate of the antagonists, Henry claimed, was in his

[7] These overtures were much more limited than has at times been assumed. See William L. Langer, *The Diplomacy of Imperialism,* ch. XXII, and the literature cited there, especially pp. 744 f.

hands. If his claim had been well founded, Henry would have been the balancer and hence the ultimate court of appeal in matters of high policy. Actually, it was a boast. But the idea did not die. Elizabeth sought to check the ascendancy of Spain by giving support to the Dutch fight for independence. James, peacock-like, forever imagined himself as arbiter of the whole world, while actually being used as a weight in the difficult balancing which the Dutch statesman, Olden Barneveldt, played before the outbreak of the Thirty Years' War. Barneveldt's fall, due to internal Dutch developments, eliminated the balancer, and the war was on for a whole generation. Within a few years Richelieu stepped into the active role of balancer, but rather to continue the war than to end it. For the military ascendancy of Hapsburg required an effective offset: Gustavus-Adolphus was hired by Richelieu to do the job.

Enough has been said to show that the balancing of powers in these early days was being promoted by an active balancer. The "great" statesmen, mastercraftsmen of the art of manipulating power, are found to be engaged in seeking balances. Why should they do this? For the sake of peace? The history of modern states suggests a different answer. Peace—at least a limited peace—may indeed be the more immediate objective, but security and national aggrandizement are behind it. As has already been pointed out, the later efforts of the British to maintain a balance and peace were rooted in their quest for empire as well as security. They wished to protect their back while their front faced across the seas. These and similar ulterior motives explain why war as well as peace may be the outcome of the balance of power.

Perhaps the worst feature of the balance of power game is the partitioning or distributing of weak links in the chain of states. This has often been done by the balancer to keep things equilibrated. Thus many of the small German principalities were parceled out between the bigger powers, Hapsburg, Bavaria, Brandenburg, Sweden, at the Peace of Westphalia (1648). The Low Countries were partitioned at the Peace of Utrecht (1713), Poland at Vienna (1815), and Africa in the course of the nineteenth century. It was this "bartering about of peoples from sovereignty to sovereignty" that Wilson protested against and wanted to see abolished. Before the war, this sort of fate was imminent for Turkey, as well as China. References to partitions of these countries recur in the diplomatic documents. Nor was the secret treaty between Great Britain and Germany for the disposal of the Portuguese colonies, or the open treaty between Great Britain, France, and a number of other powers for the partitioning of Morocco, anything else. Determined to maintain peace, the assembled diplomats at Algeciras gave little thought to Morocco. As Harold Nicolson has put it: "Behind the Morocco question loomed the essential problem of the balance of power. . . . Its effect upon Morocco can be discounted: that, at any rate, was not the main issue involved." That was in 1906. Thirty years later, British diplomats were scanning the horizon for some territory, colonial or other, which they might hand over to Germany to keep her from reclaiming Austria and thus upsetting the balance of power. They did not succeed.

Physical and Other Factors

Suppose there were only two countries in the world. Might there not be a balance between them without a balancer? Is a static equilibrium of forces out of the question? Much thought on the balance of power is vague and confused, because no effort is made to ascertain what is going into the balance. In recent years, the discussions over disarmament have brought to light the wide ramifications of this problem. Behind the size of armies and material equipment stand the industrial and other factors of national strength. Still more intangible, and yet quite real, are the moral and traditional features. Was Prussia or Austria more powerful in 1866? Mere material strength and size were all on the side of the latter, yet Prussia won quickly and decisively. A similar comparison may be made between Japan and China.

These factors of internal and external strength are by no means stable. One country may, through natural advantages or persistent effort, grow very much stronger, while another grows weaker. Does the balance of power mean that the stronger has to make contributions to the weaker?[8] The Industrial Revolution had a profound effect upon the British position in the world, as had the similar development in Prussia a

---

8 These problems are well stated by Charles Dupuis, *L'équilibre Européen* (1909), pp. 99-100.

little later. The industrialization of Russia in our time, the militarization of Italy and Germany under Fascism, all these are factors affecting the balance of power. If there were only two countries in the world, how could a balance subsist for any length of time, unless we made the unrealistic assumption that they were always moving along the same line and succeeding equally well? No, if anything is clear, it is that the power of modern national states is compounded of so many factors that to keep a group of them in balance necessitates a constant effort. Just as a scale has to be held up by some support which may from time to time have to shift its position if the scales are to remain poised, so the balance of power has to be watched and readjustments have to be made to keep it in equipoise.

The Moving Equilibrium

In some situations, the response to the growing strength of one country may be strictly competitive. The industrialization of England has been followed by the industrialization of all the world. The rearmament of Germany, itself motivated to a considerable extent by the continued armament of her neighbors and the increasing armament of the Soviets, has brought in its train an armament race of terrifying dimensions throughout the world. Responses of this kind are almost automatic, though much conscious effort enters into the practical working-out of them. By heightening the tension, such competition makes the task of balancing the powers more difficult. Armaments generate aggressive designs in the hope that they will provide some justification. Politicians, soldiers, financiers, and manufacturers, even industrial workers, combine to make up a chorus of intentional and unintentional propagandists for some victory to be won by these costly tools before they become obsolete and ready for the dump. Governments are facing a collapse of their credit on account of spending their way out of depressions and recessions by ever-mounting expenditures for arms. To more than one of these powers war may soon seem the only alternative to voluntary bankruptcy.

Perhaps some superman, some benevolent master-intriguer, could hold the scales in balance until these martial impulses have spent themselves, and one country after another is ready to return to a saner approach. But there seems to be little hope in this direction. The British government is, to be sure, still so vitally interested in the *status quo* that this idea helps to interpret their devious course. But with the whole world involved in the game, the British are no longer so effective. They cannot remain outside, as they could when they had only to maintain the *European* balance of power. Perhaps America could take over the task, but the American people have no taste for such an undertaking, so that even if the American Pitt were around the corner, he would probably have no chance to show his hand.[9]

The fact of the matter is that within a wholly inter-

9 This undercurrent dominates Livingston Hartley's challenge, *Is America Afraid?* (1937).

dependent and interrelated world everybody can try his hand at the game of being the balancer. Thus while the British may be seeking to balance Russia by Germany, Germany may be trying to balance Britain by Italy. There are in the world today a whole series of potential balances all linked with each other. Thus State A may be a balancer as regards some equilibria, while it is part of a balance in some others. Efforts at balancing the powers are at work in both Western and Eastern Europe, in the Balkans, in the Near East, in Asia, and around the Pacific. But are they successful? Can they be successful? To imagine so many scales riveted into each other is difficult. A descriptive outline of these power configurations would dazzle the mind as a kaleidoscope strains the eye. Crystallizing into ever novel combinations, these power relationships are no sooner grasped than they are gone.

The value of the idea of the balance is, under present conditions, rather slight, both for the purpose of explanation and as a guide to action. New difficulties have been added to the old vagueness. If one could object in the past that the principle of a European balance offered neither a clear nor a just solution to most international rivalries, one could damn the principle today for not offering any solution at all, either in the light of justice, or of clarity, or even of understanding. The idea of a moving equilibrium—troublesome enough in the realm of the physical sciences, with measurable, quantitative data—appears a snare and a delusion when applied to the complexities of our present international situation. Instead of order there seems chaos, instead of law, anarchy.

Federal Systems and Their Balance

Not only President Wilson but many other thinkers interested in the building of an international organization believed that a League of Nations would do away with the problem of the balance of power.[10] Their hope was the result of laying too much stress on the ideological aspect of the balance, and of paying too little attention to the real politics of leagues and federations. It is rather puzzling that Wilson, an American and a Southerner at that, should have overlooked the operation of balances of power within federal systems, and the possibility that at the breakdown of the balance, war, a civil war, became inevitable. There had been a great deal of argument in the Convention at Philadelphia over the balance between large and small states. The politics of Hamilton and Jefferson reveal the problem of a balance between industrial and agricultural states—a problem which is still with us in a very acute form. The decades before the Civil War were filled with maneuvers for maintaining the balance between slavery and antislavery states. Judge John B. Moore has written:

"What is called the balance of power is merely a manifestation of the primitive instinct of 'self-defense,' which tends to produce combinations in all human affairs, na-

10 See Theodore Marburg, *Development of the League of Nations Idea* (1932), *passim*.

tional as well as international, and which so often manifests itself in aggression. Not only was the Civil War in the United States the result of a contest over the balance of power, but the fact is notorious that certain sections of the country have, during the past generation, constantly found themselves in general relations of mutual support because of a continuing common interest in a single question." [11]

Other federal governments reveal similar problems.

If a balance of power is operative in federal systems with a clearly worked out federal government, it stands to reason that the difficulties will be even greater in a federation or league of states.[12] For here, where each component government claims independence, the maintenance of the League certainly depends upon a skillful balancing of powers. History shows that such leagues have ordinarily been held together by a common objective; they were resisting outside pressure to which the federated units were exposed in common. The Swiss cantons fought Austrian feudal control; the Dutch, Spanish ecclesiastical and commercial domination; the United States, British colonial imperialism. Even when such pressures were operative, a balance had to be maintained between the conflicting objectives of members of the federation. No one can read Hamilton's discussion of the troubles of the Confederation without being impressed with the difficulty of this task.[13] In fact, the gist of the argument in the

[11] John Bassett Moore, *International Law and Some Current Illusions* (1924), p. 310.

[12] See, for my view of the general problems of the federal system, C. J. Friedrich, *Constitutional Government and Politics* (1937), ch. XII.

[13] See *Federalist*, Essays VI-X.

Federalist is to the effect that a balancer is required to maintain an equilibrium, and that such a balancer can be found only in a sufficiently strong federal (national) authority. The Swiss reached the same conclusion in 1848, after their looser federation had dissolved in civil war. Here it was the balance between Protestant liberal and Catholic conservative cantons that broke down, because the Swiss Federation lacked an effective balancer.

It is evident that to be able to work as the balancer, the federal government ought to be stronger than the strongest of the component units. But what if some of the component units are very large? The comparative equality of the states composing the American union made Wilson forget the dangers which lurk here. Yet the dangers of the actual predominance of one or two states within a federal pattern had been acutely revealed in the German Empire. In the nice phrasing of Lowell, the federal union there "could not fail to resemble the compact between a lion, half a dozen foxes, and a score of mice." If this danger had been appreciated, the founders of the League would have been forced to the conclusion that it could not replace the balance of power, but should rather reshape and stabilize it.[14] Since the League government itself could not possibly be expected to cope with Great Britain, France, or even Italy, it was evidently too weak to be-

[14] Giving each Dominion, as well as Great Britain, a vote in the League, while helpful in "breaking up" this great power, aroused the hostility of those powers who, like the United States, looked upon themselves as equally powerful, and hence "entitled to the same number of votes."

come the balancer. Thoughtful diplomatists, like Lord D'Abernon, soon came to realize that, unless all countries were effectively disarmed and the League provided with a strong police force, "the balance of power is a condition for an effective League of Nations."[15] Already, in 1922, it had become evident that a strong army belonging to any one power would stultify the League. We all know it today. What many still hesitate to conclude is that a balance within the League is the only way of keeping the League from falling apart.

The Balance Between Insiders and Outsiders

The League of Nations as an alternative to the balance of power was conceived as a world organization. It was to be universal in its all-inclusive sway. Though a federative compound, it appeared as a new embodiment of the medieval dream of a united mankind. In reality, it was not. The Soviet Union, the United States, and Germany remained outside. Changes in the League's composition have forever left it a partial and incomplete thing. Even so, the League has not been sufficiently exclusive. It has neglected the essential requirement of homogeneity as was pointed out in discussing the League ideal. This lack of homogeneity is a matter of fact, regrettable but undeniable in a world of dictators, or oligarchies, of creed and interest. Hence there are powers outside the League, any conceiv-

---

[15] See *An Ambassador of Peace: Lord D'Abernon's Diary* (ed. M. A. Gerothwohl, 1929), II, 74, 75. D'Abernon qualifies his remark by saying that he is speaking of the balance as a "fact and not a theory."

able League. What should be done concerning them?

Surely a power like Great Britain could not be asked to carry on her foreign relations without any regard either to the United States or to the Soviet Union. Even if no balance were required within the League, what about a balance *around* the League? If the United States simplified this problem by showing no aggressive tendency, except perhaps in Central and South America, surely in the early twenties the Soviet Union, with its Third International fomenting the world revolution, was a matter of concern. We find balance of power politics, as will be shown, in the approach to these questions at the time of Locarno. In South America, balancing the influence of the United States was rarely mentioned. Yet it was a real concern of the powers, and they eventually converted their legations in the Argentine, Brazil, and Chile into embassies.

More recently, the successive departures of Japan, Germany, and Italy have made the problem of the balance around the League apparent to everybody. Even a small country, like Switzerland, is now being affected. Wedged between Germany and Italy, as well as France, Switzerland has for a long time pursued a policy of strict neutrality, guaranteed by the League. Recently, her president, M. Motta, has declared that the League seemed to be in danger of becoming a coalition of one group of powers pitched against another, and that Switzerland must seek to neutralize herself against possible emergencies. It may be doubted, however, whether the balances around the League ever amounted to a great deal. That does not alter the fact that any incomplete and partial international federation of states would have to cope with this problem, if it wanted to maintain peace. The existence of such a body never can be expected to solve the difficulties for which the balance of power is supposed to provide an answer. The balance of power may provide a temporary and unstable answer; the League provides no answer at all.

Conclusion

It is evident that international relations under either the balance of power or the league of powers are highly uncertain and dynamic. The league ideal, when coherent, transcends existing possibilities on account of the great diversity of political systems. The balance of power ideal likewise is impracticable on account of the complexity and constant change of the international alignments. There is no apparent balancer either within or without the League in its present or any conceivable reformed state. Yet, without an effective balancer, no order or balance can be expected among "independent" states. Physical and other factors are of great weight in determining the power of countries under modern industrial conditions; a vigorous government is able to utilize these resources. Hence a balance of power, though far from being a beautiful design, may yet be preferable to the international anarchy which is prevailing at present. It is a sorry concession to the foibles of human nature and the world at large. The disintegration of the belief in a natural order of any kind has quickened our desire for effective controls. If the world is a chaos of accidental configurations of matter or energy, where shall men turn for peace? Obviously, the only hope lies in the effective control of insubordinate nature. A league cannot work without a balance of power, but neither can a balance of power work without a balancer. Some sort of league is necessary as a complement for the balance, as an instrument for those who are capable of doing the balancing.

SIX

THE REAPPEARANCE OF THE BALANCE OF POWER

Vienna and Versailles

IN his *Peacemaking 1919* Harold Nicolson has told us of the spirit in which young British diplomats like himself approached their tasks. "We were journeying to Paris, not merely to liquidate the war, but to found a new order in Europe. We were preparing not Peace only, but Eternal Peace. There was about us the halo of some divine mission." In their bags, these youthful enthusiasts had a little book on the Congress of Vienna which Nicolson at least read with great care. As he reached Paris, he felt that he knew exactly what mistakes had been made by the misguided reactionaries who had contrived to build a balance of power as a foundation for peace. They had given Europe peace for a mere fifty years!

It did not take long for the work of the Congress of Vienna to appear in a more favorable light: at the signing of the Locarno Treaty, in 1925, a picture of Castlereagh, the author of the work at Vienna, was hung conspicuously in front of the tables. If, as has been said of the Congress of Vienna, the statesmen concerned were limited in outlook, too prone to compromise, lacking in faith and courage,[1] the judgment on those who made the peace in Paris has been even more severe. Following Theodore Roosevelt's sardonic advice, "Utopia or Hell!" they grasped for utopia, but gave us hell. By refusing to think about the balance of power, the Paris Conference allowed the victorious powers to impose articles of surrender upon the defeated countries. Not so the Congress of Vienna. In spite of the avalanche of violence and tyranny which had swept over Europe in the decade of Napoleon's imperial aggression, the articles of peace were the result of extended negotiations in which the government of France took a vital part. It was a negotiated, not an imposed, peace. The allies stuck by their declaration that they had fought Napoleon, not France. Hence, though riddled by imperfections, this peace lasted for over forty years. To unfold the whole sorry tale of warlike dissensions which have rent the world since 1919 would be a bitter task. The following pages sketch certain phases of this history during which the salutary effect of a measure of equilibrium became apparent.

The Polish War and Upper Silesia

The Treaty of Versailles, concluded without the participation of the Soviet Union, had left part of the Eastern frontier of Poland unsettled. Taking things into their own hands, the Poles proceeded to back an

---

[1] C. K. Webster, *The Congress of Vienna* (London, 1919), p. 148.

independent Ukraine with the result that in midsummer, 1920, the Russians advanced upon Warsaw. The Poles thereupon appealed to the Western powers for help. Owing to French intervention, the Russians were defeated and the treaty of peace gave Poland a very large part of what they had originally claimed.[2] This development squarely raised the problem of Russia's relation to Poland and the West. But it was not as yet capable of a satisfactory solution. Poland did not enjoy much sympathy in England. The Corridor, foisted upon the British against their dogged opposition, worried them; they felt that nothing but ill could come of cutting off part of Germany and in the process turning over a large number of Germans to Poland. What was more, the Poles appeared to be an instrument of French diplomacy. It was clear that the Soviets, outside and even hostile to the League, must be worked into an effective balance of power, if peace were to be maintained. But the Poles, after all, had been the aggressors. How was one to balance Poland?

This question presented itself in another setting at the very same time. Under the Treaty of Versailles, the disposition of the small but industrially important district of Upper Silesia had been left to be decided by a plebiscite.[3] The results of this plebiscite favored Germany, by about three to two, for the whole territory. But since the Treaty had provided for the drawing of a line in accordance with the vote by communes, re-

2 Lord D'Abernon, *The Eighteenth Decisive Battle of the World* (1931).
3 For details, see Sarah Wambaugh, *Plebiscites Since the World War* (1933), vol. I, ch. VI.

gard being paid "to the wishes of the inhabitants as shown by the vote and to the geographic and economic conditions of the locality," the settling of the frontier line became a matter of arbitrary discretion. In keeping with balance of power diplomacy, the British members were inclined to favor Germany, while the French members were determined that the result should be interpreted in the sense most hostile to German interests. As the French dominated the Commission, the English distrusted the result. After a considerable amount of bickering, they decided to submit the matter to Geneva "in the belief that the whole question would be referred to an independent tribunal which would hear all sides and deliver an impartial judgment. . . . Without such faith as to impartial procedure England would almost certainly not have agreed to submit the matter to Geneva." [4] But no such impartial procedure resulted; indeed, many Britishers feel with Nicolson that "the decision was, in fact, unpardonably unfair, and wholly unworthy of the League of Nations." [5]

It is from this period that men of insight, like D'Abernon, date the revival of a balance of power attitude amongst insiders of the British Foreign Office. In their opinion, the proceedings had revealed the determination of the French to maintain their hegemony through manipulating the votes in the League Council and Assembly. Whether the view was correct or not,

[4] Lord D'Abernon, *An Ambassador of Peace,* I, 22.
[5] Harold Nicolson, *Curzon* (1934), p. 212.

the logical conclusion was that the British must seek to balance the French influence both within the League and outside it.

Rapallo

Another failure of British policy in trying to deal directly with France was the London Conference of May, 1921. It convinced Lloyd George that there was no hope of achieving a durable settlement of the reparations question unless other powers were brought into the negotiations. As the United States seemed, after the defeat of Wilson, quite unwilling to respond, Lloyd George proposed to bring the Soviet Union into the international arena by holding a world economic conference at Genoa to which the Soviets would be invited. Recognition was held out to them as a bait on condition that they would promise not to engage in subversive propaganda and to respect the property of foreigners.

Unhappily, Briand's unwillingness to hold such a conference brought about his fall, January 12, 1922. He was followed by Raymond Poincaré. A British diplomatist has well expressed in what light this man appeared to many English people. "What was Poincaré's aim?" D'Abernon asked. "To make France supreme on the Continent, supported by satellite Allies in Eastern and Central Europe. Confident of English acquiescence in anything her Ally might propose or undertake; indifferent to German hostility; relying on overpowering military strength." Whether this be true or not, Poincaré certainly set out to thwart the proposed international conference. The conditions he attached to France's participation doomed it. It failed. Its failure was accompanied by a strange bit of fireworks, a convention between the two outsiders, Germany and the Soviet Union, at Rapallo.

It has been said that the Rapallo treaty resembled other Soviet treaties in being highly sensational at the time and wholly unimportant a week after. This estimate cannot be accepted in the light of balance of power politics. Since the British government was incapable of moderating the French intransigence, this gesture of Germany toward the Soviets had the profoundly irritating but nevertheless salutary effect of reminding the world that Germany might be driven to ally herself with Russia to counteract Poincaré's policy. The Soviet Union was not, to be sure, capable of balancing the British and French governments combined. She was, nevertheless, a disquieting enemy. In actual fact, the Germans repeatedly affirmed that the conclusion of this treaty did not entail an alteration in their policy.

D'Abernon, whose memoirs contain material of considerable interest on this problem, has expressed the view that the Germans were pushed into concluding this treaty by the skillful Russian diplomacy. According to this view, the Russians succeeded in creating the impression that they were just about to conclude an agreement with England and France, when actually they were anxious to exploit their treaty of alliance with Germany for the purpose of forcing an agreement from England. There were economic issues involved, particularly Germany's equality under article 116 of the

Treaty of Versailles. Under this article, Germany was conceivably obliged to pay reparations to Russia. On the other hand, Germany's action raised in France and England the bogy of secret rearmament through providing co-operation between Germany and the Soviets. That there was more than a grain of truth in that suspicion, we know today.[6]

The Occupation of the Ruhr

The remainder of the year 1922 was filled with a series of inconclusive negotiations which aimed at breaking the deadlock in the reparations issue. Poincaré moved inexorably forward in the direction of "productive sanctions," meaning a seizure of the Ruhr basin. The Ruhr valley contains the greatest conglomeration of German industry and natural resources. With most of Upper Silesia's coal and metals gone, the Ruhr constituted the very heart of the economic life of Germany. Having made a considerable effort to prevent Germany's loss of Upper Silesia, British diplomacy now sought to thwart the French aggressive designs in the West. On August 1, 1922, an endeavor was made, through the Balfour Note, to link reparations with war debts. It suggested that Great Britain "would be prepared to abandon all further right to German Reparation and all claims to repayment of her allies in respect of loans or by Germany in respect of reparations, provided that this renunciation formed part of a general plan. . . ." This move failed completely.

[6] See Benoist-Méchin, *Histoire de l'Armée Allemande—1919-1936* (published in two volumes in 1936 and 1938 respectively).

America was entirely unprepared for so generous a proceeding; England's expectation that every American should do his duty did not hold any great appeal. It must be admitted that the Note failed to offer any commensurate sacrifice on Britain's part. Without such a sacrifice, America could evidently not be enlisted for the purpose of balancing the designs of Poincaré.

The Germans also made an effort to bring the Americans into the picture. But their offer of a "Peace Pact" in December, 1922, while eliciting American sympathy, foundered upon the rock of French hostility. Poincaré claimed to be suspicious of its terms. Actually this proposal was a forerunner of the Locarno Pact. But the time was not yet ripe for so broad a solution. Poincaré was determined to push his policy of force. In his first conversation with Bonar Law, the British Prime Minister, Poincaré said: "Whatever happens, I shall advance into the Ruhr on January 15." Against such fierce resolution, the British saw no other hope than that America take definite action. Evidently, she appeared as the only hope for an effective equipoise to France. The British public were anxious to avoid a conflict, but they saw no means at their disposal. Lloyd George was probably right in feeling that public opinion in England would never stand an aggressive bullying policy on the part of France, but what could it do? The British representative voted against the motion declaring Germany in default on reparations, but when the British Prime Minister came to Paris in the early days of January, he found that "the French Premier was determined from the outset to occupy the Ruhr with or without British consent or co-operation." Were the British public ready to break off diplomatic relations and, if necessary, go to war with France? No intimation of such a course had been given by the British, and hence the French might well look upon British feelings in the matter with the same disdain which at present characterizes the Japanese attitude toward American feelings on China.

The British and French standpoints were utterly irreconcilable. But their lack of agreement did not halt the ruin of Germany's middle classes, which followed in the wake of the occupation of the Ruhr. Passive resistance, a noble gesture, completed the currency collapse; when passive resistance was abandoned, insurrection broke out in Germany.

While peace was breaking down, the League remained silent. Efforts were made to bring international co-operative arbitration to bear upon this conflict, but they failed. Slowly, reluctantly, British public opinion came to the conclusion that within the framework of international organization a predominant military power on the Continent could not be trusted to keep the peace.[7]

The year 1923 marked the parting of the ways; English diplomacy and the English public henceforth recognized that something more than the League was necessary. One finds few explicit statements of what that something was or should be. British thought and action show rather clearly that Great Britain was at

[7] See D'Abernon, II, 7 ff. and *passim*.

least glancing at the balance of power as a possible way out. For the time being, it was hard to discover what might produce an effective balance. Russia was out of the question, because of the intrinsic danger she constituted for the Empire. In fact, the British had just fought hard to disengage the Turks from Moscow, and had succeeded in doing so at Lausanne. The Soviet masters were exceedingly suspicious of Great Britain.[8] The United States was retiring into splendid isolation. As an American diplomat told D'Abernon, there might be economic collaboration, but political action was utterly out of the question. As for the small powers of Europe, the so-called succession states were satellites of France, while the "neutrals" remained neutral. Italy, however, could be drawn upon in a measure. These calculations provided the basis of Anglo-American friendliness toward the rising star of Mussolini.

But above all, there was Germany. British opinion saw that if only Germany could be strengthened and revived, a suitable counterbalance to French hegemony might be found. The following significant entry in D'Abernon's diary suggests the uncertainties surrounding this problem:

"Personally, I have always held the view that Poincaré's vaunted strength and obstinacy were based in large part upon the weakness of his opponents. . . . What has recently occurred goes a long way to show that a firmer attitude by America and England at the Hughes proposal in December, and the English proposal in Paris would prob-

[8] See above, ch. IV.

ably have avoided much that has been disastrous since. It was contradiction in terms for us to say, We disapprove of the Ruhr occupation, thinking it both illegal and injurious to our reparation interests, but we wish France luck in the adventure." [9]

It was idle to urge a firmer attitude without at the same time building a foundation for sustaining such an attitude in the face of a challenge. Here the problem of the balance injected itself.

The Near Eastern Crisis

The key to English equivocation on the reparation issue lay in the Near East. Since November, 1922, a conference to make peace with Turkey had been in session at Lausanne. The Turkish-Greek war had destroyed the basis of the earlier treaty which Turkey had never signed. British interests were seriously threatened in the Near East, and the danger of a split between Britain and France loomed. It was absolutely essential for a satisfactory settlement that Britain, France, and Italy collaborate. To maintain that collaboration, Britain had to soft-pedal the conflict over reparations. By skillful diplomacy, Lord Curzon succeeded in getting under cover the essential harvest before the storm of the Ruhr occupation broke and disrupted the alliance between France and England forever.[10]

From the standpoint of the alignments of the powers,

[9] *Op. cit.*, II, 297.

[10] See the masterly treatment of the Lausanne Conference in Harold Nicolson, *Curzon,* chs. X and XI.

the most significant result of these negotiations was Curzon's success in breaking or at least loosening the close tie between Angora and Moscow. This tie had existed ever since March, 1921. In fact, at the Lausanne Conference, Russia made herself at first the spokesman of Turkey. But Curzon drove a wedge between the two delegations. By pressing the minorities issue, he got Turkey to agree to join the League of Nations. The Soviet Union, it will be recalled, at that time looked upon the League as the "organized impotence of Geneva which serves only to further the designs of the capitalist imperialist powers." Though the idea of the balance of power is nowhere patent in these negotiations, it is nevertheless evident that Great Britain was seeking to balance Soviet power in the Near East by Turkey. At that time, when world revolution still haunted Soviet foreign affairs, the Soviet Union appeared a very aggressive force in Asia. In the Near East, as everywhere, vital economic interests were at stake which no imperially-minded government of Conservatives could venture to sacrifice for long. The enormous strategic importance of the oil fields of Mosul and Iraq made it imperative to halt the progress of anticapitalist nationalism upon which the Soviet policy was feeding. The only method short of war appeared to be to balance Russia by a tier of powers friendly with Britain. It is in this light that British policy in Turkey, Iraq, Persia, and China must be interpreted. Unfortunately, by the time this task had been accomplished, France's fatal adventure in the Ruhr had been set in motion. British policy could not undertake the task of reconstruction until France's occupation had fairly run its course.

The Dawes Plan

It is customary to describe Germany's policy of passive resistance—if a policy it was—as a complete failure. Such a judgment is rather short-sighted. It is built on the assumption current at the time, both in Germany and abroad, that it was the meaning of passive resistance to eject the French from the Ruhr. To be sure, the French were not driven out. But another and possibly more important objective was achieved. American and British public sentiment, until that time in the main hostile to Germany, swung around and commenced to assert that in conflicts between Germany and France its place was on the side of Germany. When the French entered the Ruhr on January 13, 1923, the New York *Tribune* had written:

"Germany is in contempt as well as in default. But when the conditions of the Versailles document are applied she weeps at her own misery and charges violation of compact against the nations whom she is defrauding. The irony and the pity of it are that these crodocile tears are taken as righteous anguish by persons who have never plumbed the mysterious abnormalities of the German character."

But as the year wore on, there was a gradual change of outlook. By January, 1924, even conservative circles wanted an "expert" judgment on Germany's "capacity to pay." The year 1923, according to some, witnessed the culminating point of the conflict between the policy of force and the policy of pacification. The passive resistance was decisive in focusing the attention of the entire world upon this issue. "After a desperate struggle, world opinion, slow, vague, hesitating, prevailed against military strength." Passive resistance collapsed, the German currency collapsed, but so did Poincaré's policy of force.

During the winter of 1923-24, the forces of reconstruction could gather the momentum for a counteroffensive. The result was the so-called Dawes Plan settling the reparation question. Lloyd George, at Genoa, had sought to broaden the basis for negotiations by inviting the Soviets; British statesmanship now turned toward the United States. Isolationist sentiment had prevented direct governmental action. But on the eve of the French invasion of the Ruhr, Hughes, then American Secretary of State, brought forward the suggestion for a commission of experts which might ascertain Germany's capacity to pay. This was the straw at which Europe grasped. The British worked during the spring and summer of 1923 to get the Germans to accept this suggestion. They could not press their views, because they did not want to strengthen the French suspicion that Germany was acting according to the "master's voice"—a suspicion actually voiced in *Le Temps* at that time. In the end, these efforts failed, and Germany capitulated in September, calling off the passive resistance. This seeming victory for Poincaré's policy of force turned out to be a boomerang.

Before the reaction against his policy set in, Poincaré went one step further. In October, 1923, he fostered a separatist "movement" in the Rhineland. Though presumably of popular origin, it met with the determined resistance of the overwhelming majority of German inhabitants. Bloodshed and violence accompanied the efforts of French military authorities to nurture the "movement." The British military authorities, under strict orders from London, refused to co-operate. When the French sought to shift the basis of operations to the Palatinate, Curzon dispatched the British Consul General at Munich, Mr. Robert Clive, to investigate. His excellent report was read to the House of Commons on January 20, 1924.[11] A month later the movement had vanished.

There is plenty of evidence to support the view that the firmness of Curzon was fatal to the conspiracy of the separatists. This whole scheme, though well timed to coincide with what appeared the virtual dissolution of Germany,[12] was very undiplomatic in that it suggested what had so far been only suspected: France's determination to dismember Germany. Such plans at once raised the specter of French military hegemony. Almost overnight France lost what sympathies had remained for her. French public opinion itself was slowly getting aroused over the isolation into which the country was drifting. Poincaré became very worried. Not only England, but Italy and other European countries

[11] See Hansard, vol. 169, col. 485/6 (1924).

[12] It was during the months of September to November, 1923, that rebellions broke out all over Germany; the Communists sought to establish an independent regime in Saxony; the Royalists and Hitlerites staged the Beer Hall Putsch in Munich. For much detail, see *Gustav Stresemann, Vermächtnis,* vol. I.

seemed provoked and determined that "something should be done to stop the military domination of Europe by France."

Besides these international realignments, there were domestic changes. A general election in England led to the fall of the Conservative government in January, 1924. Though in a minority, Labor took over the government. This had a profound effect upon Poincaré. He realized that he had gone too far. Besides the external balance of power, effected through bringing America into the situation, there arose the internal balance of power: a threatened shift to the Left in France.

Linked with these emerging factors balancing Poincaré's thrust at hegemony, international solidarity through the League was also being reinforced by Labor's coming into power. The British Labor party, after all, believed in the League, while Curzon had not. In spite of these differences, British reparation policy stuck to bringing America in. Hence, the expert commission kept aloof from the League. American participation was more important. During two months, February and March, the commission investigated and deliberated. Their report appeared April 9, 1924. It declared as the essential conditions of all future reparations the re-establishment of German unity, i.e., the evacuation of the Ruhr, and the discontinuance of all sanctions of any sort. Providing for a moratorium to give Germany a start back to normality, it then suggested a gradually rising amount of annual payment without fixing the total. This is not the place to discuss the details of the settlement. Suffice it to say that the plan of the experts was adopted without essential modifications. The emerging balance had done its work. The French ascendancy was checked.

Other factors were at work, too. While France was drifting into isolation, the franc declined on the international exchanges. People the world over were losing faith in French stability. Things being as they were, neither English nor American bankers were prepared to come to the rescue of Poincaré. The battle of the "golden balls" had proved more efficacious than the bullets of French soldiers in the Ruhr and Rhineland. The French public was getting restive as the French currency weakened. Poincaré, seeing himself outflanked, sought to come to terms. It was too late. Poincaré was defeated in the parliamentary elections held in France early in May, and a Leftist coalition, *Le Cartel des Gauches,* came into power. With France and England both having Leftist governments, the idea of international solidarity was temporarily revived; the balance receded into the background.

It is worth noting that at this time of crisis, France attempted to get into closer touch with Japan "to counterbalance the influence of the Anglo-American Association." This move, provoked by British condemnation of the French policy of force, was brought forward at the time England abandoned the Anglo-Japanese alliance. The Japanese turned down the French offer. Still the offer is interesting as showing that balance of power politics was making its reappearance in various quarters.

Conclusions

The foregoing reveals how the idea of a balance of power reappeared in European diplomacy after the war. Inspiring as had been the utopia of President Wilson, the real League rested upon such slender foundations that divisions within it were bound to make themselves felt. They soon revealed that federations of states are rent by balance of power politics, unless the federal authorities are strong enough to play the balancer. Such action on the part of League authorities had been explicitly ruled out under the Covenant.

British diplomacy at first made a half-hearted effort to rely upon international solidarity. But the failure of the League to act in an independent way forced professional diplomatists to realize, however reluctantly, that they must return to balance of power politics. The recurrent conflicts which arose between France and Britain over the execution of the treaties of peace made a growing number of people in Great Britain shift toward Germany. They began to feel that a pacification of Europe required that France's overpowering military strength be offset by a reconstruction of Germany. However, up to 1924, the general public in England did not realize that the balance of power was reappearing behind the League.

In other countries, the situation was not very different. German diplomats were naturally on the lookout for a possible balance which might allow Germany to escape from the fetters of the treaties. But the only power readily available for such a game was the Soviet

Union. To turn to Moscow, even for the sake of national liberation, caused the German conservatives qualms similar to those which had once worried Catholic France in utilizing German Protestants, or the Turks, in their efforts to balance the power of Hapsburg. There was a group in Germany who thoroughly believed in co-operation with the Soviets. Their views crystallized in the Treaty of Rapallo. On the other hand, German liberals and progressives had the same aversion to the idea of a new balance of power which had animated Wilson and his followers in Western Europe. Germany was too weak to take any decisive lead in foreign affairs.

France and French diplomacy had shown little faith in international organization. To them, the peace treaty had seemed to present the definite task of balancing Germany by a whole string of countries committed to enmity through territorial conflict. Denmark, Lithuania, Poland, Czechoslovakia, Italy, Belgium—they were all gainers at the expense of Germany, and hence seemed committed to a policy of holding Germany down.[13] With the support of these countries, the French commenced to develop League policy as an international extension of French policy. This was the trend against which the English became aroused. When this first began to happen, France turned to military force. Under the stubborn leadership of Poincaré, she abandoned international organization in favor of actual pre-

[13] The Allies had even tried to embroil the Netherlands, by offering them part of Frisia in exchange for the mouth of the river Scheldt, which was to go to Belgium.

dominance. But when French hegemony threatened, the rest of Europe banded together to avert it. Here, then, was the reappearance of the balance. World opinion as well as the good sense of the French people protested.

The facts proved stronger than hopes and beliefs. Beyond Europe, there loomed the world outside the League. The United States re-entered the stage, and the French thrust collapsed. Still America did not return to commit herself to international solidarity under the League. Nor did the Soviet Union.

After 1924 there was, besides the League, the balance of power as a fact. Was it to become a condition for an effective League of Nations?

SEVEN

THE PEACE OF LOCARNO AND ITS AFTERMATH

The Setting of Locarno

FOR the sake of balancing the French military hegemony in its economic effects, it had sufficed to bring forward the financial and industrial power of the United States. But there were other more purely political questions in which the aid of the United States could not be invoked. There was the problem of the evacuation of occupied German territories. There was the problem of disarmament and the League. There were the relations with the Soviet Union. These questions appeared in a different light in different chancelleries, but that they were full of dynamite no one could deny. The short-lived minority government of Ramsay MacDonald had made tentative efforts at solving them through international solidarity. Nothing was further from British Labor than a foreign policy guided by the idea of the balance of power. The Labor government had recognized the Soviet Union. It had sponsored the Geneva Protocol providing for disarmament and collective security. It had extended a friendly invitation to Germany to join the League.

Labor's political failure paralyzed the measures which it had initiated. Empire problems, like Mosul, Egypt, and India, loomed. If Britain were to maintain peace in Europe while keeping on good terms with France, if she were to avoid the position of opposing French efforts, she needed to look for a balance of forces. Likewise, if she were to check Soviet agitation in Asia, without getting herself embroiled, she could do so only by balancing the Russian forces. Such, at any rate, was the view of English Conservatives. A most revealing viewpoint is presented by Lord D'Abernon, who once wrote:

"From the point of view of English policy a big question presents itself—is a large Russia desirable? America is strongly for it, presumably as a counterpoise to Japan. English interests, I think, are much more certainly against it. As long as there is a strong Russia, India is, to a considerable extent, menaced. The Balkanization of Central Asia would be an unquestionable relief to English policy. Even as regards the Black Sea and the Mediterranean, a Russia divided into different states, whose commercial interests overpowered her political ambition, would make our position far more secure than in the event of the re-establishment of a powerful Empire. A separatist policy for the Ukraine would unquestionably lead to a safer and more healthy position in the Black Sea, and would facilitate commercial control of the Straits, as opposed to political control." [1]

This statement is, of course, no official proclamation of policy, but it shows how balance of power politics

[1] See D'Abernon, *op. cit.*, II, 99.

always plays with ideas of divide and rule. Since in 1925 the actual division of Russia was a pipe dream, it could only be a question of weakening her. And since Germany was closest to Russia among the big powers, this meant prying Germany away from her. In refusing to sign the Geneva Protocol, the British Conservatives served notice that they did not intend to jeopardize the security of the Empire in Asia by committing themselves to international procedures. They had too many doubts concerning the effective working of such procedures, because they depended upon an as yet unrealized international solidarity. From their viewpoint an equilibrium must be sought both within and without the League of Nations.

German worries corresponded to these British concerns. Much relieved by the Dawes Plan, German politics immediately turned to other complaints. Cured of appendicitis, they remembered the tumor of occupation. The French, hoping to postpone the surrender of the dead pledge of occupied territory, were raising the question of Germany's disarmament. They cited secret reports purporting to show that Germany had failed to comply, that her police forces were much larger than permitted under the treaty, that she maintained secret stores of arms in the Soviet Union, and so forth. Poincaré had advanced and Herriot, then Foreign Minister of France, had accepted the theory that in view of Germany's failure to comply with treaty provisions, the period from which to date evacuation had not yet commenced. German politicians, Stresemann particularly, were haunted by the specter of an almost indefinite French occupation. They imagined this program to be part of the French policy of keeping the Western bank of the Rhine as the frontier between France and Germany. They feared that the Geneva Protocol would perpetuate such a system.

French policy was being justified both at home and abroad as directed toward security. In German eyes it appeared to be motivated by the desire to maintain French hegemony in Europe. That granted, German foreign policy could solve its problems only by actually balancing French power and by undermining the clamor for security both inside France and abroad. By calling the bluff of security, the position of conciliatory forces inside France might be strengthened, and a new equilibrium created. For it is the balance of power at home as well as abroad that needs to be taken into account among democracies. In those efforts, German politicians could count upon a measure of support from Mussolini. For Mussolini felt himself hemmed in by republican France. He strongly objected to France's military predominance for reasons of his own. Such was the array of powers at the beginning of 1925. It was not an order in equipoise.

English or German Initiative?

Palpably the initiative leading to Locarno came from Germany. On February 9, Stresemann submitted a memorandum to Herriot, at the same time acquainting the British Foreign Office with its contents. In this memorandum he suggested an international treaty guaranteeing the Eastern frontiers of France and Belgium as well as the Western frontiers of Germany; Great Britain and Italy were to be guarantors. Such a treaty, the memorandum suggested, might be implemented by arbitration treaties between France and Germany. Germany also declared herself willing to conclude similar arbitration treaties with other powers, presumably Poland and Czechoslovakia. It was a German step, and its reception was rather cool in both England and France. Yet soon after the public was apprised of it, various people came forward and charged that the move was initiated by Great Britain. What has been said concerning the setting readily explains the charge. Nor can the question be entirely settled.

The diaries of Lord D'Abernon as well as Stresemann's papers show that the idea first developed in a conversation between D'Abernon and von Schubert, Stresemann's Secretary of State in the Foreign Office. The argument is perhaps not of great importance, but it is interesting from the standpoint of balance of power politics. D'Abernon himself has told us in his diary:

"As for my own share in the genesis of the Pact, I have steadily advocated something of the kind for the last three years. Since October I have frequently talked matters over with Schubert, more particularly after the set-back concerning the evacuation of Cologne. These conversations probably resulted in the German move of January 20, but whatever was done previous to that date was of minor importance."

Stresemann's extensive papers leave little doubt in the mind of an unbiased reader that a great deal of thought and planning in the German Foreign Office preceded the German initiative. In December, Stresemann and Schubert were already busy trying to formulate plans for countering the dangers which they saw in the Geneva Protocol and in the inclination of France and England to use minor defects in German disarmament as a pretense for staying in the occupied territories.

Stresemann himself later told the public in a press conference that the negotiations commenced in December, 1924. At that time, he pointed out, the non-evacuation of the Cologne zone was a fact and was being justified by German failure in the matter of disarmament. After questioning whether the French and English governments expected even their own public to believe these explanations, Stresemann referred to the uncertainties of the Geneva Protocol, and emphasized the dangers which the idea of a demilitarized Rhineland spelled for Germany. It seemed to revive the threat of separatism.

"We accordingly were obliged to ask ourselves whether the question of French security, this nightmare of a future German attack, all these changes in the control of the Rhineland, based as they were upon the assumption that the Rhineland is to be the region in which to draw up the troops for a future German attack,—whether all these notions could be eliminated. For they are the reasons for the continued control of the Rhineland. Such control would not be rendered any less humiliating through League execution." [2]

It was in confronting this situation that the German government had its first conversations with the English ambassador, who himself was very much taken with the idea but found London slow in responding. Chamberlain, particularly, was at first suspicious; that these *pourparlers* were initiated with such secrecy made him wonder whether they were directed against France. But the German government quickly dispelled his misgivings. Stresemann's ambassador in London declared that the German government expected to communicate their ideas to the French government at once, because "in this question France, not England, is our chief contracting partner." "If my view of the situation is correct," Stresemann added, "for the present, and for an indefinite time to come, France is not threatened by Germany, but the Rhineland is continually threatened by French Imperialism. . . ." Time has shown that Stresemann's view was not correct, but it reveals that his idea was to balance this threatening French "imperialism" by having England and Italy guarantee the frontiers between France and Germany.

The initiative then was clearly Stresemann's, and it is not surprising that when he returned from Locarno he was greeted by a telegram from Austen Chamberlain which read: "The world will never forget that it was Germany that took the initiative towards peace in

[2] See *Stresemann, Vermächtnis,* II, 66, and in the English edition, II, 64. The above translation is only slightly different from Sutton's.

Europe." Stresemann likewise considers that the initiative was essentially Germany's.

"It is often said that . . . the German Foreign Office had been directed by the English ambassador. Against this, two facts may be noted. We sounded out people and put forward feelers both in Paris and in London. . . . Twice we received hints from England not to submit the memorandum. The first hint came from Sir Eyre Crowe who said, in conversation with Ambassador Stahmer, that the German suggestions were very interesting, and that he respected their spirit, but that the English government would ask us to consider whether now was the right time to bring forward such suggestions, whether it would not be better first to settle the Geneva Protocol and various other points. When we did not react to this hint, Chamberlain told the German ambassador that he did not believe it right to proceed with such a German initiative now; the right moment had not yet come, etc. These English objections, in the course of which one of the gentlemen had, perhaps against his better judgment, admitted that he wished to carry through the Geneva Protocol, have caused us to throw our memorandum into the discussion. For these objections showed us that certain people wished to solve these problems upon another basis, that our initiative was rather uncomfortable, and disagreeable. We took the initiative in spite of it all, and it has brought us the success which we wished to secure by throwing the question of security for ourselves into the discussion." [3]

The Problem of Alsace

The Rhineland, to be sure, would be secured to Germany under any treaty guaranteeing the frontiers be-

[3] *Ibid.*, II, 113-114; English edition, II, 99. Slightly different translation.

tween herself and France. But the provinces of Alsace
and Lorraine which the Treaty of Versailles had returned to France would likewise be guaranteed to
France. Never after 1871 had the French been willing
to make a similar concession. They lived by Gambetta's
famous exhortation: always to think of it, never to
speak of it. Although these provinces had been conquered by Louis XIV and Napoleon and taken from
Germany, Frenchmen firmly insisted upon their purely
French character, and continued to talk of recovery
even by force of the lost children of France. Stresemann took a broader view. The German people, he
felt, might consider the Alsace German, but they
would not follow any government which proposed to
reconquer these lost provinces by force of arms. Besides, he felt, the disarmament made such a plan utterly impossible. So why not concede a paper claim for
real protection elsewhere?

This implied sacrifice of Alsace-Lorraine aroused the
ire of all nationalist circles in Germany. To these
critics, Stresemann replied that the great advantage lay
in securing an alignment with England against any
attack by France. There was, however, a half-conscious
shift in emphasis. It is most interestingly revealed in a
facsimile set of notes for a speech, reproduced in
Stresemann's diaries.[4] He had first put down "renunciation of Alsace-Lorraine," but then crossed this out,
and wrote "renunciation of re-conquest of Alsace-
Lorraine by force of arms, no practical importance,
but *cauchemar* of the French." Theoretically, in other

---

[4] Stresemann, *op. cit.,* opposite p. 80 in vol. II.

words, there remained the possibility of consulting the population of Alsace-Lorraine by plebiscite in order to settle the matter in accordance with the principle of the self-determination of nations. But from a practical point of view this was no great consolation to German nationalists. In the first place, they utterly disbelieved in any chance of the French ever permitting such a popular referendum, and in the second place they did not believe in such consultations themselves. After all, had it not always been recognized that a considerable part and perhaps a majority of the people of Alsace-Lorraine would vote for France? Hence, the German nationalist opposition proceeded to dub Stresemann a traitor.

The Suspicions of the Soviets

In sketching the setting for Locarno, we quoted at some length the strongly anti-Russian conception of British policy that Lord D'Abernon held. In view of such an opinion it cannot surprise us that the masters of Soviet Russia were very much alarmed by the German memorandum. Let it be remembered also that the British Conservatives had returned to power over the issue of British relations with the Soviet Union, and that they had broadened their victory by the stunt of the anti-Communist Zinoviev letter incident (above, pp. 103-104). No sooner had MacDonald made his gesture of inviting Germany to join the League, than the men in Moscow began to worry about a possible Western orientation of Germany. It had been their *idée fixe* ever since the Allied interventions that the capitalist powers were getting ready for an armed effort to overthrow the Communist regime. Sentiments like those of Lord D'Abernon did not reassure them. Hence already in September–October, 1924, they were exerting pressure in Berlin to keep Germany from joining the League. At that time Germany had issued a memorandum in which she invited comments upon two conditions which she felt must be met before she could join the League: a permanent seat on the Council of the League, and a restriction upon her obligations under the Covenant for the participation in League sanctions (article 16). Negotiations between Germany and Russia looking toward the conclusion of a new trade treaty had been lagging, too.

The misgivings concerning German policy caused Moscow to wonder whether the German government might be willing now to accept Germany's Eastern frontier as permanent. Genuine agreement between Germany and Poland would deprive the Soviet Union of its opportunity to balance Poland by Germany. The Communist party in the German parliament even addressed a formal question to Stresemann asking whether the German government had accepted the Eastern frontier. Such absurdities were denied by Stresemann with considerable vigor. In a private conversation with Tchicherin, Stresemann went so far as to say that Germany "would never voluntarily recognize the present boundaries of Poland." In a series of interviews Stresemann reiterated what he also insisted upon in public: the Russian notion that Germany was planning to develop an anti-Russian policy was completely wrong, almost absurd. In spite of the recurrence of disagreeable incidents, due to the activities of the Third International, Germany wished to continue her policy of friendly co-operation with Russia. She needed friendly relations both toward the East and toward the West.

The Russian Commissar for Foreign Affairs and his diplomats countered repeatedly that they did not expect an anti-Russian policy to be the *intention* of Germany, but that they felt that such a policy would naturally *result* from their entry into the League. In the political affairs which were of immediate concern to Germany, England would assist Germany. Her interest was to prevent France from gaining further strength on the Continent; hence Britain would help Germany in Danzig, the Saar, the question of the minorities. In turn, Germany would find herself obliged to come to the aid of Britain in a conflict involving Britain's Asiatic interests. Stresemann thought these fears were a "theoretical construction." If Russia and Britain had conflicts in Asia, they were none of Germany's business. Since Germany had been robbed of her colonies, she had nothing to do with imperialism, and had no intention of getting involved in such quarrels.

To these arguments, Stresemann added that a disarmed Germany would be of little use to Britain, even if Germany were willing to allow herself to be made into such a mercenary. Nor would France ever permit her to be rearmed. Germany must insist upon general disarmament, and for that reason could not conclude any agreements which referred to war and the possibility of Germany's participating in a war, no matter under what guise. Moscow was disturbed lest Germany be inclined to participate in League sanctions which Britain might be able to get the League to adopt against the Soviet Union. Stresemann pointed out that Germany's membership in the League also held out the opposite promise of preventing such unjust action by the League. It seemed questionable whether the Soviet Union would be the gainer or the loser. The fact of the matter was, of course, that at the time the Soviet Union generally opposed the League, just as the Fascist powers do today, and that therefore Moscow disliked any increase in the prestige and influence of this international organization.

Germany—Battlefield of Europe?

In his repeated assurances to the Soviets, Stresemann made it plain that he always had in the past and would in the future reject German membership in the League without adequate reservations regarding her obligations under the Covenant. He wanted an express limit to Germany's obligation to participate in international sanctions. At first Germany went so far as to ask for formal recognition of her special status until such time as general disarmament had taken place. Later, she modified her stand, partly as a result of British pressure. Stresemann declared himself willing to accept an especial interpretation given by the League to the provisions of Article XVI of the Covenant which would imply more limited obligations for Germany.

At Locarno, these points formed one of the thorniest

questions. It was the Germans' contention that they could not be expected to participate in any international sanctions, because their country had been fully

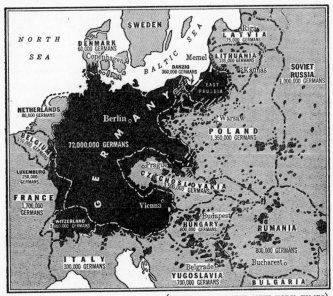

(FROM MAP IN THE NEW YORK TIMES)

DER DRANG NACH OSTEN

Black areas are claimed as inhabited by German-speaking people.

disarmed. To the argument that 100,000 men were after all a considerable army, Stresemann replied that it was needed in its entirety to maintain order at home. Particularly in any conflict with the Soviet Union, the danger of civil war would, on account of the large number of German Communists, be very great, and no part of the German army, not even a thousand men, could be spared. To the French contention that the German army, though limited in number, consisted largely of officers and commissioned officers, the Germans rejoined that the decisive problem under modern conditions was the force available at the outbreak of hostilities. Moreover, they insisted that the German disarmament had deprived Germany of the technical tools of modern warfare, guns, airplanes, tanks, etc. All her border defenses and fortresses had been destroyed, thus leaving her defenseless in a ring of neighbors bristling with arms. Under these conditions, it was adding insult to injury to blame the Germans for not wishing to participate in military sanctions under the League.

By the same token Germany could not be expected to participate in economic sanctions, for those sanctions might be considered an act of war by the opponent of the League. In that case Germany, totally disarmed, would find herself at the mercy of some highly armed and well-equipped enemy. Germany, in fact, could not even allow the armies of other countries to march through her territory, lest the fighting be transferred to within her borders. She must avoid everything which might lead to her becoming the battlefield of Europe. Germans recalled with horror the fate of their country during the Thirty Years' War (1618-1648), when Germany was laid waste in a manner which crippled her for more than a century. She had then been the victim of Richelieu's game of balancing the Hapsburg Empire, and no similar prospect could be looked upon with indifference by a responsible

German statesman, they contended. Briand argued that Germany could prevent such a situation from arising by voting against League action when the time came, but Stresemann rejected this by pointing out that Germany could not thus risk moral isolation.

For a while it seemed as if these difficulties would create a complete impasse. England was unwilling to go forward with the Security Pact without having Germany enter the League. The German contention that general disarmament was an objectively possible goal, and that with its consummation all these difficulties would disappear, encountered strong opposition from Briand.

A way out of these troubles was found by an ingenious compromise. Instead of having the League make exceptions in favor of Germany, the powers involved in the Pact agreed to interpret Article XVI in a note to Germany. In this note it was stated that regard should be had to Germany's military and geographic situation. Germany's diplomats won their point in fact, but not in form. They could now continue their policy of balancing East against West, Great Britain against the Soviet Union.

The Eastern Problems

The Locarno pacts were initiated on October 16, 1925, but a bitter fight had to be won in Germany before they could be signed on December 1, 1925. These internal struggles reveal how difficult a supple balancing policy becomes under democratic conditions. The British Foreign Office published a *communiqué* which was so worded as to imply a renunciation of territory by Germany. At this idea, German nationalist sentiment flared up and the Nationalist party forced their ministers in the cabinet to resign. Luther and Stresemann hesitated to explain their success too fully for fear that it might complicate the position of Briand in France. In the end, the battle was won; the treaties were accepted by the German parliament.

There still remained the Eastern situation. True, Stresemann had concluded a trade treaty with the Soviets on the eve of Locarno. He had also managed to avoid definite commitments concerning the Eastern frontier. Arbitration treaties with Czechoslovakia and Poland constituted a vital part of the Locarno system, but they did not guarantee the Eastern frontier. One may well ask why Stresemann, who was so insistent that use of force was out of the question, should have balked at any guarantee of the Eastern frontier. Had he not claimed also that the Western Pact did not by any means settle the frontier, but merely eliminated the use of force?

The answer is to be found in balance of power politics. In the West it was a question of bringing in England and Italy to balance France. French military strength threatened Germany with recurrent occupations, in Stresemann's view. In the East there was no such danger. The German army seemed adequate for defensive purposes against any one power. At the same time, Germany would have lost a great deal of value in the eyes of Russia, if she had no longer been available as a counterpoise to Poland. To these thoughts must be added that it was difficult enough to secure the acceptance in Germany of a treaty which was interpreted in nationalist quarters as a surrender of Alsace-Lorraine. If Stresemann had also "sacrificed" Eastern territories, he would have been overwhelmed.

In point of fact, Stresemann was far from making any sacrifice of the Eastern German territories. Indeed, in a confidential letter to the former Crown Prince, he set it down as one of the major tasks of German foreign policy to seek the readjustment of the country's Eastern frontier, the recovery of Danzig and the Polish Corridor, and a correction of the frontier in Upper Silesia. The letter, written on the eve of Locarno, aroused a storm of indignation in Parisian nationalist papers when it appeared in print in 1930. It was taken to show clearly that Stresemann was a trickster who had deceived Briand. Actually, the letter can scarcely be said to substantiate the charge. It must be considered in the light of the purpose for which it was written.

This purpose was to defend Stresemann's idea that it was wise for Germany to enter the League of Nations. He sought to convince a representative of the old pre-war order that the League could be a useful institution to German foreign policy. It was only natural for a German politician under these conditions to emphasize the League's machinery for peaceful change, perhaps even to express hope for British support. No British promises were held out at the time. But an editorial in the London *Times* calling upon Poland to make a generous gesture was taken by many Poles and Frenchmen to prove that such an understanding had been reached. Allowing for the occasion of the letter, it may even be considered doubtful whether this letter reveals Stresemann's policy. It undoubtedly shows a facet of his policy, but not its central conception. In wording many of his utterances, Stresemann had to take into account his nationalist opposition. Nowhere was this more true than in the question of Germany's entry into the League.

The Revelation of the New Balance

For Stresemann it was a ticklish matter to make plain how much it was in the interest of Germany to enter the League. He could not go very far in stating publicly how Germany could, through the League, hope to balance and counteract France. Hence his efforts to influence the opinion of important private individuals. Among the advantages Stresemann emphasized was the protection of all Germans living outside the Reich's boundaries—the so-called national minorities. Occupying a permanent seat on the Council, Germany could insist upon the enforcement of the minority treaties since these treaties were entrusted to the League's Council. Moreover, many of the questions which were agitating Germany were of concern to the League: general disarmament, Danzig, the Saar. A skillful pleader of Germany's interests in the Assembly might make the position of Germany's antagonists very uncomfortable. Nothing proved this more clearly, Stresemann pointed out, than that France was displeased at the prospect of Germany's entry. It was lucky that England should desire it to offset the dominant position of France in the League.

During the period after the signing of the Locarno pacts, the League idea steadily gained ground in Germany. On the third of February, 1926, the German government was at long last empowered by the Parliamentary Foreign Affairs Committee to apply for membership. It was the common understanding that Germany would be accorded a permanent seat on the Council.

Thoughts of counterbalancing Germany had in the meantime occurred to French and Polish politicians. A big campaign was started in Warsaw and Paris for a permanent seat for Poland to offset German influence in the League Council. Brazil and Spain had at an earlier date indicated their desire for a similar concession. Reacting unfavorably to this agitation, the German Foreign Affairs Committee now revised its instructions to the German Foreign Office. It "interpreted" Germany's application for membership as having been made on the assumption that Germany would receive a permanent seat on the Council without there being any other alteration in the composition of the Council. This instruction tied the hands of the German delegation. By opposing all alterations in the composition of the Council at the time of Germany's admission, the Germans brought out into the open the struggle over the balance of power within the League.

Even before the special meeting of the League at which Germany's admission was to be voted, in March, it became clear that France had at the outset resolved that Poland should also be given a permanent seat. Briand gladly consented to have Spain and Brazil added to the list of candidates, because, so it was alleged, he figured that it would be easier to get three candidates admitted. Also, one might be dropped, if necessary.[5] This French game met with a very hostile reception in England. Whatever may have been the views of the Foreign Office—Austen Chamberlain's stand was ambiguous, to say the least—the English public did not take kindly to what they felt was unfair play against Germany. Lord D'Abernon commented at the time:

"The more I hear of what goes on at Geneva, the more inclined I am to believe that French influence and Catholic influence there are the dominant forces. England only gets her way when public opinion at home awakes to the danger and returns a dogged 'No.' The fundamental good sense of the English people was never shown to better advantage than in regard to this matter of the dilution of the League Council." [6]

This strong reaction of the British public against the effort of balancing Germany in the League was the result of their misapprehension of the general policy. They had never interpreted Locarno in terms of a readjustment of the balance of power, as D'Abernon and other Conservative insiders had done.[7] The general public in Britain had looked upon these treaties as the necessary preliminaries for Germany's admission to

[5] For this report see D'Abernon, *op. cit.*, III, 248.
[6] D'Abernon, *op. cit.*, III, 226.
[7] See, e.g., *ibid.*, III, 199, fn.

the League, and the beginnings of genuine international solidarity. Many speeches were made both in the Commons and in the Lords, belittling the doctrine of the balance of power.[8] Surely diplomats like D'Abernon who had fostered Germany's admission expressly with a view to the balance of power in the League had no reason to be surprised at France's attempting to counter their game. They could scarcely blame France for seeking to redress the balance as much as possible in favor of herself and her allies.

When this situation became known in London, late in February, it was immediately surmised that the League meeting would end in failure. Yet, things had gone too far to postpone it. When the League Council convened, Sweden stepped forward and said "No" to any and all proposals for an enlargement of the Council. After some negotiation, Sweden offered her own nonpermanent Council seat. A compromise now seemed in sight, but Germany rejected the solution.

The German delegation greatly appreciated Sweden's idealistic view, Stresemann said later, but they were obliged to consider the realities. Their thought was that if in place of Sweden a state would be elected to the Council which was close to the Entente powers— like Poland—such a solution would be most undesirable, from a practical viewpoint. The reflection clearly gives vent to the idea of a balance of power within the League, and in fact Stresemann later said in the German parliament that their objection arose over the

---

8 See *Parliamentary Debates, Lords,* 5 series, LXIII, 284 ff. and 295 ff. (February 24, 1926), and *Commons,* CXCIII, 1120 and 1168.

political nature of the Council, which "was determined by groups, political alignments and points of view." Thus to reveal the balance of power politics behind the scene at Geneva was most unwelcome; the strong sympathies which Germany had enjoyed until then vanished almost overnight. Stresemann was well aware of it. "We realized that our stand would only with great difficulty be endured by League public opinion or by world public opinion."

There took place a further shuffling of seats; final failure resulted only when Brazil refused to co-operate in any change of the Council because her claim for a permanent seat was being discarded. To meet German objections, as well as Polish claims, Czechoslovakia had offered to resign her seat in favor of Poland, and Sweden hers in favor of another European power. But Brazil took the stand that the League Council was becoming too European. Their representative bitterly asked whether the Locarno treaties had been concluded to strengthen the League, or the League set up to strengthen the Locarno pacts? There was a good deal of resentment amongst the powers not members of the Council. They felt as Lord Phillimore did when he said in the House of Lords in February: "If we are to treat the Council as a cockpit in which people are to be equally balanced so as to have fair fights we might as well not have the League of Nations at all."

Actually, balance of power politics is inherent in a loose federation (see above, p. 133), and no matter how skillfully you attempt to screen it, the fight for predominance amongst the great powers will intrude itself. Lord D'Abernon stated the case less delicately, when he objected to the Polish claims in these words: "To contend that to have a standing quarrel with a Great Power on the Council entitles a country to a seat on the same Council is worthy of Alice in Wonderland. Admit this principle, and cats will, in future, scratch duchesses in order to be admitted to their tea-parties." [9] In truth, not even the Polish claims were at the root of the conflict: it was the balance between Germany, France, and England which was involved.

Stresemann boldly faced the real issue when he pointed out in the German parliament that a "crisis" had been brought on in the League by Germany's proposed entry. Why? Because it challenged the construction of the League as an instrument of the victors in the World War. Had not a whole range of problems come to light which had hitherto lain dormant? For these very reasons, Germany must not withdraw her application; she must continue her fight for admission as a great power. "A policy," he exclaimed, "is not wrong because its execution is beset with obstacles." The fight came to a successful conclusion in September, when Brazil's mandate on the Council expired. It did, however, entail the withdrawal of Brazil from the League. The Brazilians were unwilling to follow the example of the Swedes, of whom Gilbert Murray had rather charmingly said, "England expects every Swede to do his duty." Thus started the coming and going in the League, of which we have

[9] *Op. cit.*, III, 229.

seen so much in recent years. It reflects the shifting alignment of powers in and around the League.

The New Balance Between East and West

The alignment of powers in 1925 was such that the Soviet Union was outside the League, as a matter of course. Hence Russia's policy was one of watchful suspicion, though there were occasional rumors that Russia was seeking admission. To allay Russian apprehensions, Germany agreed to a new treaty of mutual friendship, about December of the Locarno year. The actual conclusion of the treaty did not take place until after Germany's failure to secure admission to the League in March. Still, the treaty was not the result of the obstacles encountered by Germany; its publication in April was simply due to the fact that its conclusion, agreed upon for March, could no longer be postponed. Stresemann had hoped to avoid the irritation which the Treaty of Rapallo had aroused. One of the major topics of discussion at Locarno had been Germany's relations with the Soviet Union. In a statement to the press after the conclusion of the treaty with the Soviets (Treaty of Berlin, April, 1926) Stresemann pointed out that the Locarno discussions had convinced him of English and French sympathy for Germany's desire to have friendly relations with the Soviets. Both Chamberlain and Briand had ridiculed the idea that they were tempting Germany into the League in order to make her a member of a world alliance against Soviet Russia.

When the Treaty of Berlin was made public, it

was violently attacked by conservative papers in England and France. *L'Intransigeant* went so far as to claim that the real purpose of this treaty was close military co-operation between the two countries, involving the establishment of German munitions factories in Russia, maintenance of depots, and other such undertakings. Stresemann considered this such palpable nonsense that he refrained from giving out a *dementi*. When *L'Intransigeant* was joined by *Echo de Paris* as well as the *Morning Post* and the *Daily Mail,* the German Foreign Minister felt obliged to clarify the German viewpoint.[10] The rehabilitation of Germany depended essentially upon the maintenance of a balance of power between East and West. "The policy of the German government is to combine East and West, since Germany is the obvious bridge to bring about the intercourse between East and West." D'Abernon, when hearing of the proposed treaty in March, had stated the point a bit more emphatically:

"The object in view was to maintain the approximate balance between East and West which is such an essential feature of German policy. Germany being still outside the League, it is now thought that the signature of a neutrality treaty with Russia would incline the balance too much to the East, the desire in dominant circles still being to maintain a certain preponderance of the Western inclination without undue alienation of the Eastern counterpoise."[11]

[10] See Stresemann, *op. cit.,* II, 504-11, 537-42; English ed., II, 460-67, 489-92.

[11] *Op. cit.,* III, 239.

The hesitations to which he alludes were overcome when news of the impending treaty leaked out and produced rumors which caused the German government to sign and publish the treaty.

D'Abernon's observations give another succinct indication of the extent to which balance of power politics had become re-established. The leaders of German public opinion were so profoundly convinced of the essential soundness of a policy conducted in this light that the Treaty of Berlin was accepted unanimously by parliament itself on June 10. It was a unique occurrence in the annals of German parliamentary life. With Germany's admission to the League the following September, Stresemann had become the balancer of Europe. He had been the driving force behind the building of an equilibrium which provided Germany with new breathing space. It was, however, not long before issues arose which undermined the new balance. Every balance of power system before had broken down and ended in war; how long would the new balance last, associated as it was with the League of Nations?

Conclusion

The Locarno Pact and the Berlin Treaty initiated an open effort at building an equilibrium within and around the League. A trend toward balancing the powers of Europe had been noticeable in the two years preceding. English efforts had borne some fruit, but German co-operation had carried this policy to victory. The foregoing analysis has shown how the developing of these balances was undertaken as a reinforcement to international organization under the League. It was meant to strengthen the League, not to supplant it. But the very complexity of the pattern augured ill for its endurance. What mattered from the English standpoint was the balancing of France and her Eastern allies by a stronger Germany. Within the League, French predominance might be checked. Outside the League, it was rather a matter of checking the Soviet Union. The German policy fitted this plan. From their standpoint, it was a matter of balancing France and her allies by Britain and Italy. It was at the same time a matter of preventing any complete dependence upon Britain by retaining the Soviet Union as a counterpoise. The total effect was to check French predominance in Europe, Russian advance in Asia. But all this was secondary to the revival of international solidarity. Peace, a true family of nations, seemed at long last to be re-established. This re-establishment of peace seemed at the time the great achievement. It found expression in the slogan of the "spirit of Locarno."

Were not the foundations of the Locarno pacts exceedingly tenuous? Did not a great many of the sources of conflict remain? A French author challenged the general optimism in a small volume entitled *Locarno Without Dreams*.[12] He pointed to the dangers of the situation. "The continued occupation of the Rhineland seemed a repudiation of the peace on which both sides were congratulating themselves." He insisted that France must either adopt a policy of really generous

---

12 Alfred Fabre-Luce, *Locarno Sans Rêves* (1927), published in America under the misleading title *Locarno the Reality* (1928).

internationalism, or stick to her refusal to do so. But "why humiliate a Great Power we profess at the same time to regard as an equal?" This author realized that there were great obstacles in public opinion to the course he suggested. "Perhaps we shall only have a mediocre, abject peace, maintained by threats of war, a peace in which men will be too stupid to come to an understanding, and too cowardly to fight." That sounds like good common sense today. It is the misfortune of democracy that common sense is altogether too uncommon. But was the subtle diplomacy of balancing internal and external powers able to do the work? Did the engineers of the new equilibrium manage to construct a framework flexible enough to provide solutions for the difficult problems which were theirs as a heritage from the Versailles Treaty?

EIGHT

THE BREAKDOWN OF THE NEW BALANCE

Reparation Realities

THE newly achieved equilibrium in Europe was not destined to last. The "settlement" under the Dawes Plan (1924) had been acceptable enough to Germany as long as the moratorium was in effect and while no payments were being made. Large sums of money were being pumped into Germany in the form of loans not only to the national government, but to the states, the municipalities, to industrial concerns, and even to hospitals. All in all, it was estimated at the time that a total of over six billions of marks had been loaned to Germany by April, 1928.

But as payments under the Dawes Plan got under way, with one billion marks in 1924-25 and in 1925-26, 1,280,000,000 in 1927, and 1,670,800,000 in 1928, an ever-increasing agitation for a new settlement let loose in Germany. On all sides a clamor arose that this reparation burden must be shaken off. Extremists on both sides appealed to the German income-earner, whether manual worker or middle-class professional, to denounce these "tributary payments." [1] At the same time, Mr. Parker Gilbert, the Agent for Reparations Payments, made it his business, from 1927 on, to criticize the German government budgets, national, state, and local. In these attacks he was supported by Dr. Schacht, the President of the Reichsbank. We know today that in doing this, Mr. Gilbert unwittingly became the instrument of reactionary politicians in Germany who wished to discredit the progressive Republican parties.

The course of later events has given the appearance of soundness to Gilbert's and Schacht's stand, whatever the motives behind the latter's campaign. Salaries of officials were being raised, considerable expenditures for civic improvements—playing fields, swimming pools, etc.—were being authorized, while ministers of finance loudly declared that Germany would not be able to go on paying the reparations. This looked bad, even though in substance the situation was not as yet serious. An official memorandum of the German government pointed out at the time (1927) that the 584 millions of municipal loans taken up between January 1, 1925, and September 30, 1927, were utilized to build electrical, gas, and water works as well as transport facilities. If the German economy was to expand sufficiently to meet the demands for export surpluses implied by the reparation account, surely such municipal improvements, it was argued, were part of the picture. Nevertheless, they commenced to disturb the inter-

---

[1] See C. J. Friedrich, "National Socialism in Germany," in *The Political Quarterly* (London), II, 520 ff. (1931), for a contemporary analysis.

national situation. Stresemann, who of course wished to see reparations further reduced as soon as possible, and who had to keep in mind the as yet unsettled total amount, repeatedly expressed both privately and publicly his worry and concern over these developments.[2]

People were only slowly beginning to see what some far-sighted economists had realized right along, that Germany's payment of these reparations involved a flooding of the rest of the world with German goods. The insistence upon reparation payments thus greatly aggravated the rapidly increasing trend toward overproduction throughout the world. For reparation payments brought about the building up of marginal industries in Germany. It is, therefore, not surprising that the world depression commenced in Germany. Her newly developed marginal industries were just beginning to invade the world markets. It was discovered that overproduction had reached dangerous proportions. Agitation for a new settlement of reparations intensified and began to spread abroad. Voices were even heard which demanded their total abolition.

The French became frightened. They began to worry lest a Germany freed of reparations should be enabled to prepare for a war of revenge. Hence the French sought to delay the evacuation of the Rhineland. They attempted to make the end of the occupation conditional upon a permanent settlement of the reparations issue. To such efforts Germany remained adamantly

[2] See *Vermächtnis*, vol. III, part II, pp. 255 ff.

opposed. Stresemann insisted that the evacuation of the Rhineland was Germany's *quid pro quo* for Locarno. She had a right to demand it.

At the League meeting in September, 1928, this widening breach of French and German views led to a bitter clash between the German Socialist Premier, Herrmann Müller, and Briand (Stresemann was ill at the time). Briand, in an excited speech, expressed doubts over what the government of Germany might be like ten years hence. There were forces in each people which were beyond the control of the government. This was in 1928. It was a prophetic query, indeed. But at the time it aroused bitter hostility in Germany. Stresemann felt that the spirit of Locarno was waning, that a policy of collaboration was impossible when such suspicions were harbored by the statesmen. Yet Briand, in expressing his misgivings, put his finger right on the danger spot. For the chief factor making for instability of an equilibrium among democratic governments is the uncertainty of the internal support.

The Coming of World Depression and the Young Plan

About this time, the first signs of a coming depression appeared. But the world of high finance was amazingly unsuspecting of the imminence and the magnitude of it. The British Treasury was of the opinion that a depression might be expected in Germany in four or five years. On this assumption, the Treasury felt that it would be wise for Germany to wait for a permanent settlement of reparations until then, because the depression would show people the limitations of German capacity to pay. Parker Gilbert, on the other hand, told Stresemann in a confidential conversation on November 13, 1928, that it was entirely wrong to expect a more favorable final settlement from waiting for such a depression. Stresemann was not so sure; he felt that a crisis was often the first step toward recovery. Within a year, the depression was sweeping over the world, and within three years all chances for reparation payments were gone.

In view of the facts, what importance attaches to the bitter controversies that arose over the efforts to make a permanent settlement? The importance of these controversies is precisely this, that they undermined the equilibrium which the Treaty of Locarno had sought to stabilize. It was undoubtedly a great mistake of German diplomacy to open up these negotiations. True, the difficulties under the Dawes Plan were great. But Germany had the protection of the transfer clause which would have kept the Dawes payments in Germany after international trade and credit collapsed. The premature opening up of negotiations was due to the impetuous Dr. Schacht, who did not know the diplomatic situation well enough,[3] and to Mr. Parker Gilbert, who was perhaps a little overanxious to relinquish his post before the transfer problem became really serious. These two men, in close touch with the

[3] See *Vermächtnis*, III, 383, citing a memorandum of the German government as well as letters and telegrams by Dr. Schacht. For another presentation see Hjalmar Schacht, *Das Ende der Reparationen* (1931), which attempts to saddle Stresemann with responsibility for these ill-fated negotiations. Stresemann's fault was a lack of active control, which was due to his serious illness.

masters of international finance, represented the common notion that the unsettled reparation issue was a handicap to German credit, and that a settlement would strengthen it. Actually, the commission of experts which met in Paris under the chairmanship of Owen D. Young by their extended arguments over German capacity to pay seriously undermined Germany's international financial position.

On the whole, the efforts of high finance to inject itself actively into the international situation were a failure. By their lack of appreciation of the political issues the bankers brought on a state of unrest. This eventually led to a reappearance of the economic warfare which had characterized the years immediately after the war. It should, of course, be kept in mind that very few men foresaw clearly the depression which was then so near. Economists, politicians, and journalists were all unaware of what was coming. In keeping with the curious swing of the pendulum (see ch. IV), Poincaré was back in power—had been since 1926. After he had succeeded in stabilizing the French currency, this masterful believer in playing safe was once more turning his attention to foreign affairs. At Chambéry he had said on September 30, 1928: "If it is sought to review the question of reparations, we are obliged to recall that, to be fair, whatever settlement is made should guarantee us from our debtors a clear indemnity for our war damages besides the total payment of what we owe to our creditors." He thus committed France to a course which was not really acceptable to Germany.

Wise German policy would have taken Poincaré's hint and sought to avoid the issue of reparations. But Schacht rather than Stresemann was in active control, so the German government was persuaded to place its faith in the bankers. They did not know what Poincaré knew so well, that you could not "take reparations out of politics." The eventual agreement was actually described by one of the partners of J. P. Morgan as a *final* settlement. He expressed the belief that the Young Plan, as it came to be called, made reparations a business issue. If so, it turned out to be a pretty sorry business. By the time Dr. Brüning liquidated the reparations, in the winter of 1931-32, the complete collapse of international credit was proof of the trouble which comes from pursuing such an ostrich policy. French politicians had shown how power politics can make short shrift of high finance. But this is getting ahead of our story.

What is most important to the student of international politics is that issues such as reparations and disarmament do not lend themselves to balance of power politics. They have little or nothing to do with questions of supremacy and the equilibrium of international spheres of influence. These issues are more material, more tangible, and hence intimately linked with domestic issues in each of the countries concerned.

Briefly, the English and French governments had to seek as large a payment as possible, the German government a small payment or abolition of all payments. The voter-taxpayer insisted upon this. Any agreement could only be a recognition of a temporary balance, to be upset the moment conditions would permit it. It was not, as all the high financial wizards parroted through these years, a question only of Germany's "capacity to pay," but even more one of Germany's willingness to pay. This in turn was linked with the willingness of others to buy German goods. But unless the Germans were willing to bear the requisite burden of taxes, nothing would be paid. That was the simple political logic. Poincaré knew it. Where he was wrong was in thinking that he could, for any length of time, force the Germans to want to pay such tributes. As long as the argument about Germany's capacity to pay was used, as it was used by Keynes, to combat the use of force, it was a politically useful, though intrinsically inconclusive, argument. When the slogan about German capacity to pay was used as the rock upon which to found a permanent settlement, it became a sorry delusion. Since Germany had become a democracy, no payments could continue once the people became aroused against them.

The negotiations leading up to the Young Plan were premature in assuming the German people's will to pay anywhere near the sums which the English and French people expected them to pay. They were a mistake in that they stiffened the German people's opposition to these payments. They were a calamity, because they revealed the basic clash of popular wills and the instability of the equilibrium between the democracies. Yet a measure of agreement was reached, a semblance of equilibrium preserved. For the time being, the forces of disruption and anarchy were insulated in extremist parties which seemed vainly to batter against governments ready to find compromises. But how long could that sort of thing go on?

The Young Plan was sufficiently unpopular in Germany to make it possible for the radicals on the Right, under the leadership of Hitler and Hugenberg, to organize the "Young Plan Referendum." This violent measure provided that any German who put his signature to this agreement for the final settlement of the reparations thereby committed high treason. The proposal was roundly defeated; still it was a warning of things to come. It intensified the spirit of defiance. Stresemann's policy of bettering Germany's position through a deftly manipulated balance of power was being swamped by emotional nationalism.[4] This emotionalism could not but affect the conduct of German affairs even then.

In the fall of 1928 Stresemann had, as was just pointed out, repeatedly affirmed his opposition to linking the settlement of reparations with the issue of the evacuation of the Rhineland. In a conversation with Parker Gilbert he went so far as to say that the evacuation of the Rhineland, while of great importance, was "completely inferior" to the reparations issue. In the course of the negotiations leading up to the Young Plan agreement, German policy was forced to relax. The impossibility of securing an adequate settlement, coupled with the need for justifying the reparation settlement in the eyes of as large a number of Germans

[4] See "The Agricultural Basis of Emotional Nationalism," in *The Public Opinion Quarterly*, April, 1937.

as possible, forced Stresemann to yield to French pressure, and an agreement on the evacuation was made just prior to the reparation agreement at The Hague.

In a letter of March 30, 1929, Stresemann had bitterly complained to Lord D'Abernon of the continuation of the occupation and its use as a bargaining point. If this went on, he exclaimed, he would be obliged to speak to world public opinion of the end of the spirit of Locarno. A few months later, at a critical turn in the Hague negotiations, Stresemann appealed in a private letter to Briand by pointing out that the main political argument available against popular indignation in Germany over the high annual payments of the Young Plan would be the evacuation of the Rhineland. Here, then, was a complete about-face. Indeed, Stresemann went so far as to threaten that if Briand persisted in delaying the evacuation of the Rhineland, he would not be in a position to put his signature to the Young Plan, "because this plan rests upon a unity of the political and economic questions." After some further protracted negotiations, the date for the evacuation of the Rhineland was decided upon just prior to the understanding concerning the Young Plan for reparations; the two agreements were formally concluded on August 30 and 31 respectively.

In spite of thus allowing reparation and evacuation to be linked, Stresemann had succeeded in appreciably bettering the conditions of the "permanent" reparations settlement suggested by the experts in Paris. Still, the German opposition pounced upon the terms of the Young Plan with rasping indignation. They denounced the German "slavery," the tributary "bondage" which had been agreed to for two generations. Up and down the land orators declaimed, protested, vilified. Hatred descended to the incredibly mean slogan: *"Stresemann, Verwese man."* (Stresemann, you should rot!) Is it to be wondered at that Stresemann himself cited the evacuation agreement as a main argument in favor of the Hague settlement, that he caustically commented on the nationalists' failure to appreciate this achievement? But though he had done his best, it could not be denied that Germany had found herself obliged, under continuous protest and at the cost of violent opposition at home, to sign a new treaty, the provisions of which could not possibly last once a depression unsettled international trade and finance. The Young Plan was a stop-gap, a harbinger of more trouble yet to come.

The Struggle for Disarmament

Another rock upon which the new balance foundered was the issue of disarmament. Ever since the conclusion of the peace treaties, disarmament had been a skeleton in the closet. It has been shown how vitally disarmament is related to an effective international organization. As long as there are nations which can defy international solidarity by buttressing themselves behind a powerful military machine, the problem of how to balance those powers remains, whether within or without an international organization such as the League (see above, pp. 136 ff.). Hence, the real believers in the League made continuous efforts at pushing disarmament. These efforts, though receiving much lip service from all quarters, did not show notable results until governments sincerely sympathetic with the idea came simultaneously into power in England and France. 1924 marks the beginning of a real effort, culminating in the Geneva Protocol.[5] Attempting to put teeth into Articles VIII and IX, this League resolution never came into force.

The Protocol was killed by a combination of British and German opposition. In October, 1924, the Conservatives returned to power in Britain. They were disturbed over the implications of the Protocol for the Empire. Communist influence was rapidly spreading in China and other parts of Asia. The Soviets were outside the League and increasing their armaments very rapidly. At first, the Conservatives merely hesitated. It was not until the next spring that Austen Chamberlain openly rejected the Protocol and brought forward the idea of regional pacts. But it is clear that from the start they were casting about for something more limited and less risky all around than disarmament. The Germans were apprehensive for other reasons. It was part of the Protocol plan to put German disarmament under the League. Stresemann and the inner circle of the German Foreign Office feared that this would result in permanent arms inequality for Germany. Any agreement made on this issue without Germany seemed to them an agreement against Germany. It would perpetuate, even sanctify, the French military hegemony

---

[5] See above, pp. 106-107. Cf. also J. P. Baker, *The Geneva Protocol* (1925), and the *Journal Officiel* of the League for the discussions.

in Europe, Stresemann felt. The German initiative which led to Locarno was born of these apprehensions. It triumphed over the broader idea of the Protocol. Though theoretically sound, the idea of the Protocol had proved premature.

Talk of general disarmament came up at Locarno just the same. In connection with Germany's reservations about Article XVI of the League Covenant (see above, pp. 172 ff.), Stresemann suggested that general disarmament was practical under the League. Briand disagreed, saying that "those nations which would be faced with the duty of defense would be obliged to assume the burden of large armies." To this principle of general inequality, the Germans strenuously objected. As Luther put it, the Germans "must expect the League to introduce general disarmament which would provide for a minimum of troops for every state, but a relatively equal minimum." In keeping with these views, the final protocol of the Locarno Conference stated that the Pact would hasten disarmament. The signatories pledged themselves to collaborate in the League efforts and to seek a general understanding. These formulae suggest the coming conflict. The German formula of equality henceforth was opposed to the French formula of security.

In his first speech before the League, Stresemann sounds the new note. "The complete disarmament of Germany is laid down in the Treaty of Versailles as the beginning of general disarmament. May we succeed in making some practical progress towards general disarmament!" The demand for equality was soon to become an effective argument against attempts to delay the evacuation of German territory on account of "minor" violations of the German disarmament. More and more insistently the German voice was raised in Geneva on behalf of general disarmament:

"We have before us a promise solemnly given to the world. It has become the moral basis for the League of Nations. This promise states that the disarmament of the vanquished nations shall be the condition for the general disarmament to follow. If you attach any importance to the faith in great ideas, if you believe that they play a rôle in the progress of nations, then do not deceive the faith which has been put upon the sanctity of the birth certificate of the League of Nations!"

Repeatedly, the German Foreign Minister professed this faith, and offered his country's eager participation in all work furthering the general disarmament. He went so far as to claim that Germany needed security more than any other country. The German public expected disarmament and would criticize a government which failed to press for it. The American people were likewise decidedly in favor of it. The sessions of the League were increasingly dominated by this problem.

This is not the place to consider the endlessly complex technical aspects of disarmament.[6] What matters is the continued agitation. In 1927 the Dutch sought to revive the Protocol, criticizing at the same time the

[6] See J. W. Wheeler-Bennett, *Disarmament and Security since Locarno, 1925-1931* (1932). A really comprehensive study of the political, economic, and diplomatic aspects of the disarmament problem since the war remains to be made.

"Concert of Great Powers" which seemed to manipulate the scene. Their proposal was defeated. But the Preparatory Commission was urged to speed its labors so that a General Disarmament Conference could soon meet. In the meantime a general declaration in favor of peace was adopted, the Briand-Kellogg Pact. Acclaimed at the time, it has turned out to be an empty gesture. Pious rhetoric can do little to resolve the deep-seated conflicts between nations. To call this bluff, the Soviets came forward with a proposal for total disarmament. Journalists in Europe and America were quick to see the meaning of the sardonic gesture. Action of some sort seemed overdue. Yet Conservatives in Britain and France were equally slow to respond; the Locarno balance did not work.

Patently, disarmament presupposes co-operation, not competition. It is not a question of balancing, but of pooling power. Agreement has to be reached, but the first condition for compromise is a willingness to come together and agree. That willingness did not appear in Britain until, in 1929, Labor once more took over the government. Unfortunately, a similar change did not occur in France. Although Arthur Henderson, as representative of Britain, made persistent efforts, the Disarmament Conference did not meet until June, 1932. By that time, the shadows of resurgent German nationalism were falling across Europe. The silhouette of Hitler loomed on the horizon. Though the Conference opened with an impressive blowing of trumpets, it never got anywhere. Perhaps if Dr. Brüning could have continued at the head of German foreign affairs, some results might have been achieved. But, although the calling of the Conference owed not a little to his skillful diplomacy, he was regrettably displaced before the meetings began.

It is in many ways puzzling that the Conference met at all that year. It was undoubtedly in part due to plain inertia. There was also the devastating spectacle of the world depression burdening every government with mounting relief costs. No one had as yet thought seriously of spending his way out of the depression by a governmentally financed armament boom. Instead, governments were playing with the idea of fiscal relief through disarmament. The Hoover government eventually went so far as to make the suggestion of a slash of one-third in the armament budgets all around. Nothing came of that idea, either. Working through cumbersome committees, the Conference negotiations meandered through the maze of technicalities, until the rise of the Swastika overtook their ill-starred labors. No one today would claim, however, that by any conceivable method of procedure the Conference could have succeeded, things being as they were.

The willingness to grant Germany her insistent demand for formal recognition of her right to arms-equality waned as the German governments following that of Brüning appeared in the thinly disguised garb of military dictatorships. "We hesitate," said the British Foreign Secretary on November 10, 1932, "from anxiety as to the use which might be made of the new situation and from fear of the resulting dangers which might threaten the tranquillity of Europe." That the German

(LE MATIN)

THE GENEVA CARNIVAL

THE ANGEL OF PEACE: *I know you, pretty masks.*

delegates should under such conditions quit the Conference was to be expected. So England, France, and Italy gave in, on December 11, with a declaration that the Conference should be guided by the grant to Germany of equality of rights. This principle was to be embodied in the conclusions.

When the German delegates returned, Adolf Hitler was about to come into power. That Hitler should, on May 17, 1933, offer complete disarmament revealed the solemn mockery of a long-lost hope. "Germany will disband her entire military establishment if other neighboring countries will do likewise." The German *Führer* thus echoed the insincere call completely to disarm which Stalin had voiced in 1928. It was the considered opinion of competent observers that "France and her allies regard Hitler and his Nazis as too great a threat to justify them in going in for disarmament at this time" (New York *Times,* September 17, 1933). Though some further face-saving efforts were made by France and England during the fall, Hitler walked out on them on October 14, 1933, slamming the door behind him. He undoubtedly knew that he was kicking a corpse.

Austrian Anschluss?

There was another major complaint of German democracy against the peace treaties: the German minorities living abroad. Presumably protected by international treaties, they nevertheless had many grievances. The German government found it hard to aid these "German brethren"; yet their plight found a ready echo in the nationalist press of Germany. What-

ever ill befell them seemed an accusation against the
"self-determination of nations." Stresemann's efforts
to precipitate League action had foundered upon the
united opposition of England and France. Neither
government cared for the issue; themselves fairly
united, these nations preferred to let sleeping dogs lie.
But the minorities were not really sleeping; incessantly
they bayed at the doors of Germany (see above, p.
81). The German minorities in Poland exerted continuous pressure. They had not yet lost all hope of returning to the Fatherland.

The problem of the relations between Germany and
Austria was similar. Immediately after the war, "German" Austria, governed by Social Democrats, had
been expecting to join with the Reich presided over
by Comrade Friedrich Ebert. Indeed, the two countries had provided for a union in their new constitutions. The peace treaties categorically forbade such an
Anschluss of Austria. Was Germany to emerge from
the war more formidable in man power than she had
ever been? The thought terrified Lloyd George no less
than Clemenceau. So when it turned out that Austria,
a heart without a body, could not live, the Western
powers endeavored to help her—not without forcing
her to promise to keep her "independence."

There was a good deal of opposition to unification in
both countries. In Germany it was feared in certain
quarters that Austria, predominantly Catholic, would
make Germany a Catholic country. In Austria, traditionalism and Catholicism combined in opposition, because they worried over the Leftist, Republican orienta-

tion of the Reich. While Stresemann was in power, the issue never emerged. Hard-headed politician that he was, he could see much trouble, little gain in unification. Surely, any move in that direction would frighten France, he reasoned, and upset the equilibrium upon which his policy rested.

By 1930, much had changed. Moderate conservatism was governing Germany; the Catholic leader, Dr. Brüning, was battling a depression at home, mounting French antagonism abroad. The equilibrium of the Locarno days was falling to pieces. Austrian finance was on the brink of disaster, French bankers pressing it to surrender. In both Germany and Austria, violent nationalist opposition was attacking the governments for their weakness, demanding action. In this desperate situation, the two governments took a bold step. On March 22, 1931, they announced that three days earlier they had agreed at Vienna to the establishment of a customs union. France had been advised two days before the announcement, and a trial balloon had been let off in a leading paper. Still, this action burst upon an unexpectant world like a bombshell.

Though couched in terms of an economic agreement, it immediately resulted in a political storm. Here was the act of bad faith the French nationalist opposition of Briand had been waiting for. Mockingly, it was pointed out that during the very days when the Germans were negotiating in Vienna, Briand had been telling the Chamber that the danger of *Anschluss* had passed. French papers professed to be appalled at the shattered balance of power. No German protests, emphasizing the purely economic character of the proposal and pointing out that other powers were welcome to join the suggested customs union, were of any avail. "The project aroused the states of Central Europe, particularly Czechoslovakia; it provoked misgivings among all powers who watch over the maintenance of the European order and equilibrium; a united Central Europe menaces this equilibrium by establishing German domination." Comments like this were one more proof, German journalists bitterly rejoined, that many people with callous naïveté denounced every sign of German life as an attack against the order of the world.

The veritable press war of mutual recriminations which followed clearly revealed the extent to which the balance of Locarno had broken down. The German government, for obvious internal and external reasons, abstained from denying that the customs union was a step toward *Anschluss*. At the same time it insisted upon the purely economic character of the project. The French government, after a half-hearted attempt at minimizing the danger, agreed with Senator Bérenger that "this audacious initiative was threatening the European balance of power." France, the Senator alleged, was trying to maintain such a balance against the forces of imperialism, new-born or reborn. In a Foreign Affairs Committee session, Briand was reported as saying that the step was contrary to the rules of European collaboration. They had been just about to discuss at Geneva the better organization of Europe. All that seemed endangered now. Those who had undertaken this step, Briand exclaimed, had no right to do so, and he intended to prevent them from going on with it. "Plainly a halt has been called in our relations with Germany. . . ."

Once more, the popular "wills" of Germany and France were at loggerheads. No open conflict ensued. The machinery of arbitration under the League sidetracked the issue, backed as it was by the power of French international finance. Even before the World Court declared the proposed customs union unlawful, the Austrian government withdrew the project. The self-determination of the Austrian nation had once more been thwarted in the name of international order and law. From the French point of view, the balance of power, though seriously impaired, had been salvaged. It was to be the last time.

This analysis would not be complete without two epilogues, one financial, the other personal. Consequent upon the failure of the Brüning government in Austria, German and international credit collapsed; so did the policy of Aristide Briand. The hopes of the Briandist group to see him President of France were devoured by the vultures of French nationalism. But this was merely incidental to the discrediting of his entire foreign policy, based as it was upon playing the balance of power game within the framework of the League, with Germany as a partner as well as an antagonist. Briand was no fool, as the French chauvinists pictured him. He made the first real effort at democratic foreign policy in France. He failed only because the issues confronting him were getting beyond democratic control. A retreat of the forces of co-operation was turning into a rout. The hurricane of world depression swept all efforts at co-operation away. After Briand's death, in the spring of 1932, a liberal-minded, intelligent Frenchman remarked to the author: "The Germans have killed Aristide Briand!" That was mistaking the dagger for the murderer. Like Stresemann, Briand died exhausted in the fight to bring democratic order out of the barbed-wire entanglements of the peace settlement of 1919. He could say proudly: "As long as I am here there will be no war." Now he was dead. So much for the personal obituary.

The financial epilogue to the ill-fated customs union was equally tragic. On May 11, 1931, the Austrian Creditanstalt, the largest banking firm in Austria, failed. The attempts of the government to deal with the resulting crisis were blocked by France. She demanded that the Austrian government write Paris a letter in which Austria was to declare most solemnly that in the future she would abstain from all combinations of a political or economic nature which could alter the international status of Austria. Only upon receipt of such a letter would Paris permit the League to give assistance to Austria. Such was the "independence of Austria" at this time. English intervention enabled Austria to reject these extortionate conditions. It was a Pyrrhic victory. A fortnight later came the chance for France to get even with England and Germany. The German banking crisis brought forth the Hoover "moratorium proposal": all international payments, including reparations and debts, were to stop for one year. It was a desperate and last-minute move; everything depended upon quick action. But the French delayed, hesitated, objected. By the end of July, 1931, the entire international credit structure came tumbling down.

The End of Reparations and Debts

In 1931, Dr. Hjalmar Schacht published a short book entitled *The End of Reparations*. In its closing paragraph Schacht declared that unless the world cooperated in a program which would enable Germany to sell her products abroad and thereby earn the payments agreed upon under the Young Plan, reparations would come to an end. He felt that the Allies had assumed a moral obligation to provide Germany with favorable conditions for selling her products abroad. What Schacht proposed was an international financial syndicate which would enable backward countries to buy producers' goods on a large scale. He realized that with shrunken markets due to the depression no country would be willing to open its doors to large German imports; hence new markets must be found. If they were not found, he insisted, Germany must cease paying reparations. As we have just shown, the international credit structure collapsed in the summer of 1931. The Hoover Moratorium, originally intended to stay this collapse, went into effect in August.

Would Germany resume the payments at the end of the moratorium period? In *Reparation Reviewed* Sir Andrew McFadyean has concluded that the Young

Plan was not, in its essence, a final plan.[7] Since control of the transfer was placed in Germany's hands, Sir Andrew argued rightly that a suspension of transfer meant a re-examination of Germany's capacity to pay. It must, however, be remembered that this transfer protection applied only to part of the annual payments; 612 million gold marks were to be paid under any and all conditions for thirty-six years. Financial experts believed that these payments might be converted into private ones by mobilizing the capital sum through international loans and thus permanently settle them. The idea belongs to the days before governmental currency exchange control ended payments on private loans as well. Mobilization meant that those Americans unwise enough to subscribe to such loans would pay the interallied debts, instead of the American taxpayer. The latter would have had to foot the bill if the debts had been canceled. After the debts were in effect canceled, no more such loans were made.

In fact, the world depression closed all these hopeful avenues of approach. The world's markets were contracting at a disastrous rate, and only those bold enough to believe in their understanding of the business cycle were willing to venture upon remedial suggestions. "Bankers may issue manifestoes, League of Nations Committees may preach the true gospel and pass resolutions,—it is all dismissed as academic; every country has its Balbus, with a vested interest in the multiplication of walls. . . ." This remark struck out with par-

---

[7] P. 202. Cf. the discussion in "The Young Plan in Operation," *Proceedings of the Academy of Political Science,* XIV, 2.

ticular force at the United States. The Young Plan had made it clear that "Germany is being taxed for nearly two generations to enable the rest of the world to pay its debts to the United States" (McFadyean). It seemed clear to all but the people of America that some day either tariffs or debts must be abandoned, because in the long run payments between nations must be made in the form of goods. If European observers thought that there was hope for such insight becoming generally accepted in America, they were sadly mistaken.

In the eyes of American common folk the debts payments remained a moral rather than a political or economic question. This attitude sprang from the American people's remorse at having been drawn into the war. "It was not our war; let them pay who profited by it." No balance of power could cope with these democratic sentiments. To give counsel, as had been done at the time of the Dawes and the Young plans, seemed all right. To give that kind of arbitral service, the United States could be persuaded; even if acting only informally, America had co-operated so as to counteract French policy. But to surrender claims, though they were mere paper claims—no. Herbert Hoover and his friends, the international financiers, might appreciate that "a great empire and little minds go ill together, and generosity in politics is not seldom the truest wisdom." The people would have none of such wisdom. Hoover's leadership was suspect, discredited by the depression. Might he not be the dupe of Wall Street, trying to save its foreign loans at the expense of the taxpayer? "If the British can't pay, let them say so. . . ." Well, the British would not, unless the Germans said it first. Calmly, the Germans did it.

On January 9, 1932, Dr. Brüning let the cat out of the bag. First came a quaint "indiscretion" by the British ambassador to Berlin. Then followed a more specific statement by the chancellor that Germany not only could not, but did not want to pay. It was an audacious move. There were men in France who wanted to reoccupy the Rhineland. That might have meant war. Hence parliamentary leaders in Paris refused to permit reoccupation, if the Germans were to resist. To a confidential inquiry from the French ambassador, as to whether the Germans would offer armed resistance, Dr. Brüning gave a noncommittal answer. The French recoiled. England and France did not, could not, act. "Any gesture of violence must be discarded," wrote *Le Temps,* counseling reason and calmness.

The policy of complete cancellation of reparations, initiated and developed by Chancellor Brüning, was formally consummated in the Lausanne agreement in June. According to the official British version, an arrangement was there signed under which Germany would be substantially relieved of a burden which had become intolerable. The participating creditors agreed among themselves to a waiver of their intergovernmental debts. This "arrangement" the British considered provisional and dependent upon a satisfactory settlement in respect of the debts for which the creditor powers were liable to the United States government. In fact, the arrangement turned out to be final, in spite of the fact that a satisfactory settlement was never reached. But it was not long before Great Britain, true to the original Balfour Note of 1922, approached the United States with a view to cancellation of the debts. In an elaborate memorandum, dated December 1, 1932, the British set forth the reasons for their conviction that a resumption of war debt payments "would inevitably deepen the depression in world trade." The United States remained unmoved. Debts had to be unilaterally abandoned just as reparations had been. In the place of law and rights, brutal facts emerged.

Violence to the Fore

The increasing turmoil in the Western world, the breakdown of the balance of power and of international solidarity, had not gone unnoticed in Asia. Japan, long covetous of extending her dominion on the Asiatic mainland, disturbed by Chinese hostility to "collaboration" and by the growing military strength of the Soviets, seized this favorable opportunity to strike. Distraught by the depression, facing a presidential election, the American administration did not wish to act without the British. The latter were tied by the European situation, and hesitated to move. The failure of the American government to respond in the debt situation was a stumbling block. So the Japanese moved ahead, made war upon China without declaring it, defied the League, and set up an independent Manchuria.[8] Not only the balance of power, but law and

---

[8] See Henry L. Stimson, *The Far Eastern Crisis* (1936).

order altogether were breaking down in the Far East; violence came to the fore.

Would the same thing happen in Europe? Hitler stepped into the chancellorship on January 30, 1933. Unrelated to any immediate external crisis, this fateful event occurred in response to internal difficulties which need not concern us here.[9] But the change in Germany immediately injected itself into the international situation with the most far-reaching consequences. Would Germany be able to continue her efforts at balancing France by the Soviets and the United States? Would she be able even to stay in the League to carry on the game of international collaboration? Would she be able to retain the friendship of Great Britain? It did not take Hitler long to return an emphatic *no* to all these questions. The work which the depression had commenced Hitler completed. At first, he hesitated. The threat of a combined French and Polish invasion terrified him. At the same time, the French were afraid of war with Germany. They feared war, because it was war; the Nazis dreaded it, because they knew they would lose it. Posterity will look upon this situation as fantastic.

The new masters of Germany felt sure that the French would start a preventive war; they went to extreme lengths in trying to pacify and mollify the world. They knew their own minds and their plans. "There is only one way for the French to escape, and that is to fight us now," said a leading Nazi to the

[9] Although much has been written about these events, it is clear that the entire story of Hitler's coming into power has not as yet been told.

author in May, 1933. "To avert this catastrophe, extreme sacrifices must be made," Hitler repeatedly told his lieutenants. But when the French did not come, the Hitlerites decided that France was down and out, decadent. In judging thus, they were wrong. France did not want to fight a war to avoid a war. You do not jump into the river to escape from the rain.

But France did something else; she returned to the policy of prewar days. Hitler did practically nothing to prevent this shift. Indeed, he aided it unwittingly. Oblivious to the foreign policy needs of Germany, he denounced the Soviets because they were Communists. A revived Franco-Russian alliance was the result. Hitler quit the League and the Disarmament Conference; the militarists and imperialists in France and in Britain took new courage. His policy of rearmament did not frighten them; perhaps it even cheered them. What were the natural resources of Germany compared to those of France, England, Russia, the United States? Hitler persecuted the Jews with ferocious pedantry. Democratic America, sensitive because of her own racial difficulties, ceased to buy German goods. Germany's international trade rapidly declined all over the world, her credit disappeared.[10]

Gone was all appearance of international solidarity, gone was the hope of an effective balance within the League. Instead of a concert of powers holding the French military superiority in check, a system of alliances made its appearance to thwart the danger of

[10] This critical interpretation of Hitler's foreign policy is shared by Dr. Max Beer, *Die Auswärtige Politik des Dritten Reiches,* 3 ed., 1935.

German expansion. Though the British Conservatives were distrustful of Moscow, they could not deny that an alliance between France and Russia was worth experimenting with. Further to confound Hitler, the British seized the occasion of the Nazi uprising in Austria to draw Italy into the new alignment. Within the short space of a year, Germany had lost almost all the gain in diplomatic position which she had slowly achieved under the Republic. As before 1914, she faced a hostile and overwhelmingly strong group of powers. Instead of being in the center of a flexible equilibrium, as she had been after Locarno, she was alone, isolated, distrusted, feared. Would Hitler be able to extricate the country from the quagmire into which his views had plunged German foreign policy?

Prelude to Anarchy?

Like every modern government, the Nazi government of Germany strove to buttress its international position by propaganda. In fact, Nazi propaganda went beyond anything that other powers, except perhaps the Soviet Union, had undertaken. But the aggressive program which Hitler had laid down in his autobiography, *Mein Kampf,* made it rather difficult for such propaganda to succeed. It is very important in all international propaganda to find slogans with a general appeal to which the specific policies of the country can be linked. The Nazis really possessed only one such slogan, their crusade against Bolshevism. There can be no question that this idea had considerable appeal in certain quarters. Unfortunately, it deepened the apprehensions of the Soviets and removed any doubts they previously had concerning effective collaboration with the League of Nations.

It has been shown how the League in the days of Locarno appeared to Moscow in the light of a hostile combination of capitalist powers bent on destroying the Soviet Union. But the rise of the Nazis convinced the masters of the Soviet Union, or at least the dominant part of them, that they must break with this conception. Remembering the lesson of the war, the slogan of democracy was revived. However grotesque may appear the Stalinist dictatorship's pose as the defender of popular government, it was certainly no more so than the Czar's participation in the struggle to make the world safe for democracy. This combination, though experience had shown it to be fatal to German interests, had been re-created by Hitler's foreign policy. To seal the realignment of powers, the Soviet Union was admitted to the League of Nations in September, 1934.

Did this regrouping of the powers represent a new balance of powers? Can we, particularly in view of later events, conclude that these were the beginnings of a world alliance system in which Fascist and anti-Fascist powers were balanced against each other? Such a conclusion could only be reached by those who have a mechanical conception of the equilibrium. In the light of our general analysis (above, ch. V), such a confrontation of two hostile camps is not a balance, but a preparation for war. It is, to be quite frank, the prelude to international anarchy. For the balancer is lacking, the engineer who, without being committed to either side, can hold the balance and prevent a struggle.

Conclusion

Contrary to the hopes entertained at the time the Locarno treaties were concluded, the balance within and around the League proved untenable. Perhaps an equilibrium cannot be manipulated between democratic nations without giving them a common superior, a true federal unity. At any rate, the attempt to strengthen the League and international solidarity by a balance of powers miscarried. Analysis shows that this breakdown of the new balance came gradually. Certain international issues of immediate concern to the masses of the people, like reparations, debts, and disarmament, found the British and French people as victors confronting the Germans as the vanquished. These were issues which like business deals follow the Red Queen's "the more there is of mine, the less there is of yours." Compromises proved difficult, and when reached resembled stop-gaps. Perhaps an active American foreign policy could have stepped into the breach as an effective balancer, if the American people had been willing—as they were not—to sacrifice the war debts for international leadership. The world depression further widened the rift.

The complete breakdown of the Locarno balance was revealed when the Austro-German customs union was proposed. Here was unilateral action challenging the partners to the Locarno Pact, rather than maneuvering them into acceptance of such an augmentation of the power of Germany. It was natural that a cry should be raised against it as a threat to the balance. What balance? Actually the proposed customs union merely brought to light that there no longer was any balance. Like the Morocco crises before the war, this initiative showed that Europe was in danger of being divided into two hostile camps. This trend toward division became even more marked when Germany proceeded to declare the end of reparations. For she was soon followed by England, France, and other powers announcing the end of war debts. In the place of law and rights, there emerged, as we said, brutal facts. Americans could do little more than tell themselves with a shrug of the shoulder: "Tu l'as voulu, Georges Dandin."

What little hope there might have been for the rebuilding of a new balance of power, after the festering sore of reparations and debts had thus surgically been removed, was destroyed by the appearance of Hitler. Through his policy of denouncing East (Soviet) as well as West (France and the League), he soon brought about the emergence of a hostile front of anti-Fascist powers. All that remained for his blundering statesmanship was to seek as best he could to build a front of Fascist powers to oppose it. This is not balance of power politics, but a relapse into the international anarchy which existed immediately before the World War. The rapidly mounting armaments on all sides testify to the fact that we are facing not an equilibrium guaranteeing peace, but the crisis before a war.

NINE

INTERNATIONAL CIVIL WAR

The Specter of 1914

HISTORICAL analogies are risky. At times they become dangerous obsessions. To see the world today in terms of 1914 is quite misleading. In 1914, a great war broke out, but few men had expected or feared it. Today, everybody is afraid of such a war, anticipating it, talking about it. So far it has not come. The conflict has taken the form of a civil war with international complications through foreign intervention. The great powers bombard each other and sink each others' ships, but they do not declare war. Many leaders constantly avow their horror of war. Even the Fascists and Nazis, though glorifying war as a wonderful trial ground for virile manhood, seem to be afraid of it, at least for the present. To be sure, Mussolini attacked Ethiopia, but then . . . so did the British subdue the Boers, the Germans the Herero in South-West Africa, and all the "civilized" nations together triumphed over the Boxers in China. These colonial "adventures" of European imperialism were bloody and cruel, but if they were wars, they belong in a different class, be-

223

cause they were never contests between equals. Who would claim that Mussolini's undertaking in Ethiopia was? Real, dangerous war has so far been avoided, in spite of all the saber-rattling. There is a burnt smell in the air, just the same.

Upon closer scrutiny, the psychological situation appears almost a complete contrast to that prevailing in the spring of 1914. At that time, although there were a few well-informed people in high positions who worried about the coming of the war, most ordinary men lived in a state of blissful unawareness of the impending disaster. News of the murder at Sarajevo, which in retrospect one knows to have been front-page news, was tucked away on an inside page in the London *Times*. There had been a softening of the tension between England and Germany. A general spirit of optimism prevailed. At no time since the philosopher Leibnitz had proclaimed this the best of all possible worlds had so many people been inclined to agree with him. There had been an almost unbroken increase in wealth and welfare in all major countries. The expectation of bigger and better things to come was prevalent throughout the world.

Today gloom pervades everything. The general spirit of the leading nations is at a low ebb. The enthusiasm of the dictatorships remains forced in its violence. It is a symphony in blue, indeed. Everyone is afraid of war, real, devastating war, in a way unknown in 1914. At that time people had to go back a generation or more to recall the memories of war. The bitter sorrows had faded into pale shadows; patriotic legend had adorned the past with romantic tales of heroism. Today war is still a living terror in the minds of many men. At the helm of affairs are those who were active participants in the fighting during the World War. Even a man like Hitler has found strong words to condemn war. "Nothing we know of could justify the renewal of such a slaughter. . . ." No doubt he was speaking with an eye toward the public, but that merely emphasizes the point.

In the light of this psychology the position of governments all over Europe is more uncertain than in 1914. Governments then could count upon the loyalty of their people. There were the occasional rumblings of radical pacifists. Some Socialists had dreamed of calling a general strike to prevent the outbreak of war; behind this idea were notions similar to those animating the sponsors of the Ludlow amendment. The propaganda and excitement generated by the approaching crisis drowned all such sentiments. When the call to arms came, most men responded. The Third Republic appealed to French radicals to defend civilization against the militarism of the Kaiser. The Kaiser proclaimed that he no longer knew any parties and recognized only Germans; his appeal to German Marxists to defend themselves and their country against the autocracy of Czardom swung German pacifists into line. In Russia, Socialist leadership was scattered, banished to Siberia, exiled to Switzerland. Even remote America eventually marched "to make the world safe for democracy." The masses everywhere followed their governments and gave them solid support. They accepted the official propaganda version of the nature of the conflict. As the struggle wore on, however, internal unity cracked. It happened first in France, then in Germany, and finally in Russia. The French army revolts were drowned in blood. In Germany, Leftist opposition demanded peace and governmental reforms; eventually the revolutionaries took over the government. In Russia, the whole social order collapsed, Communism triumphed. These events, fresh in the memory of all governments today, make war appear very dangerous.

It is generally acknowledged that at present neither France nor England would be able to call up their people to fight, except to repel invasion. This fact weakens both governments diplomatically. Yet I believe that in a long-drawn-out war these countries would again prove superior in fighting morale to Italy, Germany, and Russia. In fact, not one of these dictatorships seems in a position now to face a sizable war; the collapse of general morale would be likely to occur within a rather short time. One should never forget that in these countries considerable opposition persists. That opposition would, of course, seize the chance to turn their guns upon the hated rulers. It is the nemesis of governments built largely on force that they easily crumble under pressure, even though they are enthusiastically supported by their party following. The genius of Napoleon I could not avert this fate. Will Hitler be able to do it? In spite of appearances to the contrary, the world is today largely composed of nations with weak and poorly supported governments.

This quite obviously creates a situation not comparable to that in 1914.

Two Hostile Camps

The uncertainties in the internal affairs of most nations are paralleled by confusion if not by chaos abroad. It is common to think of Europe as divided into hostile camps. This was the situation before the war. Two large power blocs confronted each other, the Triple Alliance and the Triple Entente. They were believed to be evenly matched, and the war showed that they were. Since 1904, when England was drawn into the Franco-Russian orbit, there had been little change in this stable line-up. Even though Italy slipped out of her engagement with the Central powers and joined the opposite camp, the war probably would have ended in a stalemate if the United States had not entered it.

Today, Europe is again divided into hostile camps, but these camps are ill-defined; they cut across nations and create the setting for civil as much as for foreign war. Hitler is openly committed to the idea of a bloc of Fascist powers, the powers of "order," as he chooses to call them. Stalin is similarly committed to the idea of a bloc of anti-Fascist powers, the "democratic" powers, he calls them. But the real powers of order and democracy, America and the European neutrals, as well as Great Britain, are very uncertain about the whole conception of these fronts. Indeed, they are recurrently engaged in rather half-hearted efforts to break up the hostile camps. At the time the Austrian Nazis staged their *Putsch* against Dollfuss and murdered him, the imminent danger of *Anschluss* called forth the Stresa Conference, which seemed to align Italy with France and England. Again, the German abandonment of the League and her resumption of armament brought the Soviets into an alliance with France, accompanied by rather unconvincing gestures toward the introduction of democracy into Russia.

Mussolini's adventure in Ethiopia completely wrecked the Stresa agreement, and the crusade against Trotskyism has revealed once more the despotic violence of the Muscovite rulers. Hence there can be no question that Hitler's conception of a Europe divided between Fascism and Communism is dominating the scene. The most decisive factor has been Italy's imperialism. It will be a long time before the complete story of this amazing enterprise will be known. Certain features are clearly recognizable. At first Mussolini evidently had reason to expect that the British and French would acquiesce in his plans. These governments had been rather callously offering concessions in return for Italian co-operation against Germany. But in making these concessions the British and French governments had gone forward without adequate regard for their public opinion. Particularly in England a great deal of indignation was aroused by Mussolini's imperialist gestures, as he prepared this "war"; there were also strong protests from India and South Africa. Hence Great Britain began to gather courage, and by the fall of 1935 she was clearly at odds with Italy. It is essential to realize that Mussolini wanted the war. Offers of colonial concessions did not meet his needs. As

Borgese has said: "For ten years, after having stamped down all lawfulness in his own country, Mussolini had crawled around the ramparts of international law searching in vain for an inviting breach. Now he stood up, defying openly all guardians and tearing in their faces a file of pledges and treaties." [1]

It is common in England and America to suppose that concessions can be discovered which will satisfy the Fascist powers so that ever after you may live with them in peace and quiet. This idea is quite wrong. A man like Mussolini wants trouble. A dictator lives by tension and strife. When, preceding the Ethiopian adventure, Sir Anthony Eden suggested a compromise with Mussolini by which Italy would receive a part of Ethiopia, while the Ethiopian Emperor would be compensated by a concession of British colonial territory, Mussolini is said to have emphatically rejected all such ideas. After the interview he is reported to have exclaimed: "I never saw a better-dressed fool!" Eden reciprocated, so the well-authenticated story goes, by telling friends that there was no living with a fellow like Mussolini. The only thing to do was to get rid of him. Presumably in 1938 Lord Halifax had a similar experience in Berlin, as did several British intermediaries before him. Trying to find the basis for a compromise, he was met by a volley of demands from Hitler. In short, there is no way of reaching a settlement. Even an olive branch is, in Borgese's picturesque phrase, a thorn in the dictator's eye. When in trouble at home, he strikes abroad.

[1] G. A. Borgese, *Goliath—The March of Fascism* (1937), p. 404.

No balance can prevail against bellicose aggressiveness, except through war. The pusillanimous efforts at stopping Mussolini through the application of League sanctions could not succeed without being backed by a

(FROM LE RIRE)

What Next?

determination to fight. Counting upon timidity, Mussolini decided to bluff. He knew, as he himself later admitted, that an oil embargo would have killed the whole adventure.[2] So he threatened war, if the embargo were imposed. Britain, not feeling prepared to fight, did not dare to call his bluff. This, at least, is the official legend. In fact, it seems incredible that those in power in Britain and France did not know that Mussolini had neither the will nor the power to wage war

[2] See Marshall Badoglio's volume *La Guerra d'Etiopia* (1936). It contains a significant preface by the Duce.

against them. Had he not threatened war when sanctions were to be applied? Had he not likewise threatened war when the British fleet was concentrating in the Mediterranean? And had he not backed down both times? Again, can it be imagined that the British Intelligence Service, usually so efficient in finding out the most secret movements of an enemy, had no knowledge of the Italians' plight? To ask these questions is to answer them. What then could have motivated the British in adopting the policy they followed? Why did they so persistently refuse to apply the oil sanctions? In order to answer this query it must be remembered that it was after all an imperialist, Conservative government which was ruling Britain.

The Conservative government's backing of the League was never so unqualified as the popular sentiment in favor of collective security. The British government also had to take account of feeling in the dominions, which was strongly pro-League. The Conservatives, particularly the Right-wing inner circle concerned with imperial and foreign policy, never felt quite at home with this League enthusiasm. Throughout this volume, we have had occasion to discuss their doubts and hesitations. They saw the Empire threatened at points where the League could not help. In the early days it was the Soviets outside the League which made the League seem unsafe. More recently, it was the Soviets inside the League. There were many among the Conservatives who sympathized with the continuous assertion of Fascist and Nazi propaganda: "Either black or red, either Fascism or Communism!"

The same slogan now was brought forward. What would the government of Italy be after Mussolini fell? We can be certain that the Duce assured British Tories it would be Communism. Other Italians were none too specific. The risk of a Communist Italy was bound to appear formidable in Tory eyes. The British government recoiled.[3] Mussolini was allowed to go ahead and wreck the League and international order. The anarchy was on. The division of Europe into two hostile camps was becoming clearly visible.

It is not surprising that Hitler grasped the opportunity which this development suggested. Behind the smoke screen of the Ethiopian campaign Hitler could proceed to scrap the disarmament provisions of the Versailles Treaty. In the spring of 1935 he reintroduced universal conscription, and openly announced a policy of rearmament. There were protests from Britain, France, and the League, but no more. This encouraged Hitler to try a more daring step. The dissensions between Britain and France over sanctions in the spring of 1936 emboldened him to reoccupy the Rhineland. In justification he claimed that France's alliance with the Soviet Union had violated the Locarno Pact. Besides being an excuse, this also was a reminder to timid British Conservatives of dreaded Moscow. A delightful bit of irony in view of Stresemann's Treaty of Berlin,

[3] The idea of unpreparedness came in as a handy excuse. What was more, it could be made the entering wedge for asking popular support of increased armaments. This interpretation is supported by Arnold Toynbee's massive documentation in *Survey of International Affairs*, 1935, vol. II, even though the author makes an understandable effort to "explain" the British position as well as possible. See also his striking analysis of the rearmament policy in the volume for 1936.

which Hitler was still maintaining! Reports have it that both the Army and the Foreign Office in Berlin were firmly opposed to the move. We are told that the reoccupying troops had orders to withdraw, if the French should march. But Hitler presumably knew, through Ribbentrop, what the Army and the Foreign Office, dealing with Eden, did not know: that the Right-wing conservatives would not support any vigorous action which might lead to war.[4] So the French did not march. They felt that they could not afford to do it without British aid.

Again the question presents itself: Why did the British government fail to act? Surely, they must have known the disagreements and uncertainties which preceded the step. Besides, it did not require great powers of divination to see that the Germans would back down if confronted with action instead of words. But only words followed. It was, of course, as easy as in the Italian case to deceive the man in the street by asking: Do we want to go to war over this issue? What, after all, is the demilitarized Rhineland to us? But the question did not present itself thus to the men in the know. Hence, we can but assume that the Conservative reactionaries in this situation, too, were guided by their fear of Bolshevism. Had not Hitler's propaganda time and again brought forward the idea that the Nazis had saved Germany from Communism? Was it

---

[4] It has been alleged that Hitler was tipped off as to the probable decision of the cabinet by an English lord belonging to the reactionary, pro-Fascist group in the Conservative party. One hesitates to name this individual, though the identity of this friend of democracy is an open secret amongst insiders.

not true that the only opposition—underground, of course—which remained in Germany was Communist opposition? So terrible a risk could not be taken. Germany had once before, in 1919, been on the brink of Communism. Never again. Thus the specter of the two camps worked behind the scenes. The imaginary danger of civil war and revolution forestalled any action which might have curbed the progress toward war and international anarchy.

Considering the increased international tension, the gains of the Hitler government were rather meager. The main benefit they derived from this coup was an enhanced prestige inside Germany. It was also argued that the French could no longer effectively support Czechoslovakia in case of German attack. This contention was not well supported by military evidence. Rather it was a matter of making such support more dangerous and costly. Against this advantage must be set the increase in suspicion against Germany and the tightening of the alliances against her.

Religious War—an Analogy?

To dispel any doubts which might have existed in the minds of cautious people as to the division of the world into two hostile camps, Mussolini and Hitler next threw themselves vigorously behind the rebellious forces of General Francisco Franco in Spain's civil war. Here at last it could be demonstrated beyond any reasonable doubt that the world was divided into blacks and reds. As the Survey of International Affairs has put it:

"By the close of the year 1936 the National Socialist makers of German policy and opinion professed to see the menacing shadow of a titanic Russia spreading over the whole of Europe from Moscow to Prague, from Prague to Paris and from Paris to Madrid, while non-German [read non-Fascist?] eyes were at least as acutely and uncomfortably aware of the shadow of a gigantic Germany spreading as far as Seville and Melilla in one direction and as the Ukraine and the Urals in the other." [5]

The inclination to magnify the Russo-German rivalry must be tempered by the realization that both those powers as well as Italy are continuously harping on the complete and irrevocable division of the world into two hostile camps. Nobody expounded this more explicitly than Adolf Hitler himself when he declared at Nuremberg on September 14, 1936:

"Here we actually have two different worlds . . . which can never be brought together. . . . It is not our fault if Europe is divided into two parts; it is Bolshevism that has attacked the principles of our whole human system of the state and of society, our culture, our beliefs, our morality. . . . We believe that, sooner or later, no nation . . . will be spared from making a last clear decision. . . ."

Statements of this kind were merely the verbal framework for the vigorous support which Hitler and Mussolini gave to the Spanish Insurgents. Equally real succor came to the Loyalists from Moscow. There can be little doubt concerning these facts, however uncer-

[5] Arnold J. Toynbee, assisted by V. M. Boulter, *Survey of International Affairs, 1936* (1937), p. 9.

tain one may be regarding the origin of the Spanish troubles. It may be a long time yet before an impartial observer will be able to determine with any measure of certainty whether it was the Russians or the Germans and Italians who were the first offenders in Spain. There can be no doubt at all that these three powers were ready to stand by their own partisans in this fratricidal struggle of the Spanish people. Perhaps nothing illustrates more strikingly the abyss which separates our contemporary world from that of 1914. Continuous acts of war have been committed, fighting has been openly admitted and gloried in by the respective dictators, any of which would have plunged Europe into a general war prior to 1914. In short, war has actually been carried on by several of the great powers under the guise of the Spanish civil war. Such a situation was utterly unimaginable in 1914. Indeed, one has to go back a long way in the annals of European history to find a parallel to our present chaos.

Since the establishment of the modern state system in the seventeenth century, wars have been largely governmental wars. Perhaps there were conflicts approaching the present pattern at the time of the French Revolution and the first Napoleon. Considered in all its aspects, however, the Spanish civil war is without precedent within the last three hundred years. Even the English civil war was fought out largely by the English alone. Only at the beginning of the Thirty Years' War do we find a situation analogous to what we are witnessing now. In 1618, the Protestant Bohemian Estates revolted against the Catholic Emperor-

d a Protestant, Frederick of the Palati-
w of James I of England, on the throne
This act set the spark to a conflict which
moldering for many years. It brought the
tween Catholicism and Protestantism to a
setting the previous distribution of power in
Europe. The result was that all of Europe
the ring with men, money, and munitions. At
st, it was all done very clandestinely, but as the civil
war developed, it became more and more apparent that
all major powers were participating. Yet at the time
no one, except a few astrologers like Kepler, foresaw
that this civil war was the beginning of thirty years of
bloody strife which was to lay waste the larger part of
Central Europe.

The reason for the spread of that local civil war may
be found in the deeper nature of the conflict. It was
the clash between religious faiths, between rival ideologies, which urged the contestants on and on. The uni-
tary religious pattern of the Middle Ages had been
effectively broken by the Reformation. For decades the
strife had been flaring up in different countries, sometimes remaining purely local, at other times involving
foreign intervention. Certainly the Dutch struggle
against Spain could never have been carried on without continuous aid from France and Britain. Both these
powers were anxious to weaken the might of Hapsburg, so they helped the revolutionaries. But for special
reasons not to be discussed here the conflict did not
spread. Similarly the Spanish conflagration may not
spread. One should not overemphasize, perhaps, the

analogy to our time; for the condition
Europe before the Reformation were certa
from those of the nineteenth century.

Like all historical comparisons the anal
the period of the religious wars and the pre
an approximation. But there is an important
a fundamental pattern of unity has been destr
yond repair. In the sixteenth century it was a p
system resting upon religious faith, while today it
one built upon secular social beliefs. Surely there are
great differences between pure religion and the beliefs
of man about social order and justice. But they have
this in common, that they arouse in their believers a
fanatical attachment and an inclination to look upon
their opponents as subhuman. The ferocity of the religious wars was due to the fact that men believed the
other side to be agents of the devil.[6] It was an act of
piety to destroy such fiends. In our time, when many
men's vital beliefs are focused upon this life instead of
the life beyond, conflicting social philosophies arouse
equally powerful feelings of brutal lust for annihilation. The spirit which animated the Protestant pam-
phlets about "popery" in 1600 now lives in the Communist literature about capitalist exploiters. And when
the Nazis talk about Communist "bloodhounds, beasts,
and *Untermenschentum,*" they echo the feelings which
abound in the denunciations of the detested heretics by

---

[6] See the stirring panoramas painted by Hans Jacob Christoffel von
Grimmelshausen in his immortal *Simplicius Simplicissimus.* This epic
of the Thirty Years' War should be required reading at the present time
for all dabblers in dogmatism and civil war.

outlook for the future is dark.

To the anxious query: Is there go...
Europe? the answer must be that it has a...
Perhaps in 1966 we shall be looking back so...
to the year 1936, knowing that in that year the second
Thirty Years' War commenced. There is no use in
deluding ourselves into thinking that peace prevails,
when practically all Europe is engaged in fighting,
even if the fight is so far being carried on in Spain.
For there is no telling when a similar situation will
crop up elsewhere. After the immediate Bohemian
conflict had been decided in 1620 by the victory of the
Imperial and Catholic armies at the battle of the
White Hill, the stringent acts of retaliation and plunder
committed by the victors soon led to a new flare-up
elsewhere. This went on from one theater of war to
another, until the final draw of utter exhaustion was
reached in 1648.

Today Spain is by no means the only country in
which civil war is conceivable. Old Bohemia, now
largely Czechoslovakia, may again become the battlefield of the rival camps. It is dangerously placed between Germany and Russia. Recent events have accen-
tuated the precariousness of her position. It is unlikely
that the Czechs will surrender without fighting, as the
Austrians did. Hitler's ambitions for breaking up their
country are much more likely to take the form of an
armed uprising of the Nazis in Czechoslovakia. A re-

bellion like that could then be supported much as the rebels in Spain have been supported by Hitler and Mussolini, while the Soviets would probably seek to bring aid to the Czech government. Indeed, it looked for a long time as if the Austrian situation would develop along similar lines. Schuschnigg's frequent assertions that he and his supporters would fight certainly lent color to this prospect. But evidently the clerical dictatorship of Schuschnigg did not enjoy sufficient popular support to venture upon a life-and-death struggle. Probably the Austrian army also refused to fight. In Czechoslovakia this might all be different. The Czechs, more stolid and effective than the easygoing Viennese, even though hampered by the presence of large numbers of German Nazi sympathizers within their midst, seem determined to defend their hard-won national freedom to the last ditch. The international civil war between Fascist-Nazis and Communists may well flare up next in Central Europe.

The Rome-Berlin Axis

The "ideological" conflict has been greatly aided by the notorious Rome-Berlin axis. This dangerous piece of architecture has been cemented by the common risk Italy and Germany have been taking in Spain. Lying straight across the Moscow-Paris axis of the Popular Front, it has proved more real than was at first supposed. For quite a while it seemed rather vague and more suitable as an instrument of propaganda than diplomacy. But Hitler's invasion and seizure of Austria revealed the axis as more than that. Evidently, the

the hero slaying the international dragon of Communism. As for the Nazis, the axis greatly increases Hitler's chances for playing his game of intimidating blows. These thrusts enhance his power and maintain his prestige. The simile of the axis well epitomizes the imperial pretensions of the two dictators; it suggests that Europe revolves around their "iron wills" for order.

The general understanding between Germany and Italy differs basically from prewar alliances. In spite of what was said during the war, it is clear today that the alignments in Europe at that time were essentially defensive. Indeed, the one act clearly resembling recent events, Austria-Hungary's seizure of Bosnia and Herzegovina in 1908, occurred outside the prevailing alliance system. It resulted from a bargain struck between Vienna and Petersburg, and was sharply criticized by the respective allies. William II flew into a rage at this breach of international law.[7] But neither he nor England and France could stop what had been agreed upon between their respective allies, after it had become a *fait accompli*. It is, of course, possible that the Berlin-Rome axis will eventually turn out to have been no more than a defensive alliance either. The known facts speak against this interpretation. The course of the Spanish civil war clearly reveals active

[7] See, for a thorough analysis, Bernadotte E. Schmitt, *The Annexation of Bosnia* (1937).

co-operation in aggressive designs. In open defiance of their international commitments, Mussolini's Italy and Hitler's Germany intervened with arms, men, and money to support the cause of Franco. It is generally admitted that without this aid Franco's armies would have been crushed. Whether that be true or not, there can be little doubt that they were strengthened considerably by this Fascist-Nazi support.

Italy and Germany have continually insisted that their support was necessitated entirely by Soviet support for the Loyalists. They have keenly resented what support the Blum government gave the Loyalists at one time. From a conservative legal viewpoint support of the Loyalists bears an entirely different complexion. Anyone familiar with the issues which arose during the American Civil War will recognize the difference. Italy and Germany solved this difficulty by recognizing Franco's as the legitimate government of Spain. In this way, the Fascist general was more advantageously situated than the American South, whose strenuous efforts to secure recognition from Britain and France failed. There was then no common ideology to fight for, such as binds the Fascist powers.

The Rome-Berlin axis really is the small side of the triangle Rome-Berlin-Tokyo. Held together by an anti-Communist pact, these three militant regimes constitute a sufficiently powerful combination to be able to defy international law and order at their pleasure. On the surface the pact is rather innocuous. It provides merely for concerted action in checking world Communism. The Japanese went so far as to tell the Soviet

that the pact involved no military
ance. Yet, soon after it had been concluded (November
26, 1936—between Germany and Japan), the Japanese
started to invade North China. Their avowed purpose
was couched in smooth oriental phrases; behind them
clearly stood the determination to conquer and hold
large parts of China under the pretense of uprooting
"Communism."

Repeatedly, the Japanese had demanded that the
Chinese government take up the cudgels against this
movement which "endangered the peace in the Far
East." The protectorate which the Soviet Union had
established over the Peoples Republic of Outer Mongolia had for some time given the Japanese cause for
alarm. The military propagandists continually referred
to Moscow as a menace "glaring across the frontier
with the eyes of a tiger." [8] There had been a rebellion
in the Mongol province of Manchukuo, and the Soviets
had concluded a mutual assistance pact with Outer
Mongolia, after declaring that they were prepared to
defend the frontier of Mongolia by force of arms.
Fearful lest Stalin extend his sphere of influence further into central China, the Japanese have gone forward with the conquest of China; and the Russians
have been supporting Chinese efforts at resistance to
the best of their ability with arms, ammunition, and
money. Meanwhile, the British have completed their

[8] Quoted in Toynbee, *op. cit.,* p. 930.

naval base at Singapore and American college girls have burned their silk stockings. In short, there is one more theater of war between Communism and Fascism. It continues to be warfare on a large scale, with the democracies looking helplessly on.

The Japanese have repeatedly denied that they are taking part in any ideological conflict. What they mean to avoid thereby is the impression that Fascism is fighting democracy: that would not fit in with their desire to remain on good terms with the United States. That they are participating in a fight of Fascism against Communism, as Hitler and Mussolini see it, the Japanese can scarcely disavow. To be sure, the Japanese ideology for maintaining the ruling classes in power is linked with Japanese traditions. The situation has been described quite succinctly and definitively thus:

"The collision between Japan and Russia in North-East Asia was no less an impact of cultures and of national philosophies than of material interests. In their expansion to the mainland the Japanese were actuated not only by a desire to enlarge their territorial empire, but also, as was made clear by much that was being written and said in Japan, by the conviction that Japan had a 'mission' to propagate her cultural ideas among the local populations, and to give the lead in a movement towards a spiritual renaissance of the Asiatic peoples, which implied, incidentally, a reaction against the influences of Western Civilization. In Communism the Japanese saw a rival influence which presented the chief obstacle to the successful accomplishment of these aims." [9]

[9] E. G. Hubbard, in *Survey of International Affairs*, London, 1937, p. 936.

the European Fascists to mobilize traditional elements of national culture and religion in order to buttress the threatened control of a privileged few. To be sure, Communism has a somewhat different flavor in China than in Germany or Italy. For it is only natural that the peasant masses of China should wish to resist the rapid extension of that feudal species of industrialism which is so characteristic of Japan. That they should, in this struggle, be willing to avail themselves of the aid of Moscow means something akin to Germany's policy after Rapallo. But China was actually disintegrating. The split in the Kuomintang seemed, for a while, to seal the breakup of China into a Left-wing South, ruled from Canton and closely in touch with Moscow, and a Right-wing North, ruled from Nanking and closely in touch with Japan. Continued Japanese pressure brought about a reunion along a middle-of-the-road compromise. Surely, the Kuomintang under Chiang Kai-shek is no more Communistic than Germany was under Ebert and Hindenburg. But the Japanese claimed to be fearful that reunited China would fall under Soviet domination. They pointed with alarm to the Chinese student Communists. Do the students at Bennington prove that the United States is on the brink of a Communist revolution?

While every detached observer knows that these charges and countercharges of Communists and Fascists are made to stir up unrest, they play their sinister role in inflaming passions just the same. They make the setting required for the outbreak of "ideological"

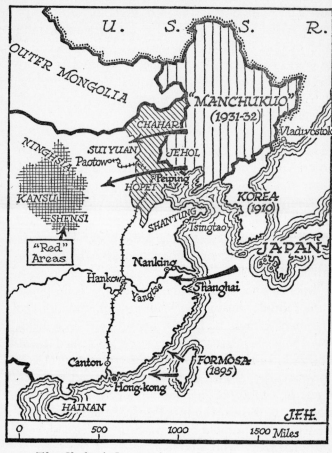

The Clash of Communism and Fascism in China.

From *An Atlas of Current Affairs*, by J. F. Horrabin,
Alfred A. Knopf, Inc.

wars. The Rome-Berlin-Tokyo triangle or axes enclosing the Soviet Union's center of world revolution is the visible symbol of the international civil war into which the world has been plunged since 1935-36. Any effort to split these axes must address itself not only to the interests, but to the ideologies as well.

Pax Britannica?

The attempt to combat this creeping pest through League sanctions ended in failure. As has been shown before, the League powers stopped short of applying the decisive oil sanctions. Mussolini completed his conquest of Ethiopia rapidly enough to prevent the more limited sanctions from having any appreciable effect. French conservative opposition had something to do with it; British Tory fears had something to do with it; America's not being in the League also contributed to the failure. During the Spanish civil war and the invasion of China, the League proved even more helpless. About the Austrian collapse, it remained silent altogether. In the face of this utter breakdown of collective security, British imperialists reasserted the idea of *pax Britannica,* of maintaining world peace by the might of the British Empire. Had not the British Empire served this purpose throughout the nineteenth century? To many who were convinced of the need of force in government, a strengthening of the Empire seemed the only hope.

Pointing to the apparent threats of Mussolini during the Ethiopian crisis, and to the even more palpable German militarism, the British Conservative government initiated a vast program of armament. It over-shadowed anything the continental dictators outside Russia had ever been able to envisage. This was accompanied by a wave of military expenditures all over Europe. Down to the smallest neutrals, governments have sought to finance larger armies and navies. Even the United States has joined the general rush. Once more, the whole world is returning to the old discredited adage: *Si vis pacem, para bellum.* Behind it all stood the fierce aggressiveness and will to expansion of the dictatorial regimes. Ethiopia, Spain, China, Austria . . . they are successive links in a chain of demonstrations illustrating the impossibility for even the most amiable man to live in peace when it does not please his quarrelsome neighbor.

The tortuous complexity of British foreign policy can only be comprehended if the reawakened imperial will to power is taken into account. We need not approve this, but we must recognize the fact. We hear time and again that if America and Great Britain will stand together, they can keep the peace. This formula, though superficially attractive, might draw the United States into a situation where she would have to defend British imperial interests. These interests are threatened all over the world. Consider the Far East. Britain's attempts to balance the Soviets by Japan may have been undertaken in the interest of peace. They have facilitated militarist aggression by Japan on the Asiatic mainland. Today this aggression has reached proportions endangering the British Empire itself. But can the Empire fall back upon Moscow to balance Japanese imperialism? Such an idea terrifies any good Tory cabinet, both for what close co-operation with the Soviet Union might mean for the Empire, and for the repercussions of such a move at home. Of course, if the Americans were, or had been, willing to fight for the Open Door in China, it would have been fine. But they won't do it. So there is nothing left, except to prepare for war in the hope that the might of empire will repress the budding Caesars.

To the great distress of British imperialists, the Italians and Germans have learned some lessons from Stalin. If the Communists have taken it upon themselves to stir up the masses in the Far East, in China, in India, in Persia, the Fascists have concentrated on the Near East and Africa. Mussolini has had the impertinence to proclaim himself the protector of all Islam, and to broadcast throughout the Near East what the British describe as "scandalous lies." He has been fomenting trouble in Egypt and all along the North African coast. He may even try to get hold of Iraq—he would not have to worry about oil sanctions after that. In all these activities, the Germans have assisted. Trained propagandists have been sent into these lands, as well as into the former German colonies to organize not only the German settlers whom a lenient democratic policy after the World War had left in possession of their plantations, but even the natives. Politically alert leaders among these subject races are realizing more and more clearly that the struggle between the several white nations is offering them the opening wedge for effective resistance to colonial imperialism, "the white man's burden."

All this is sad to contemplate for those who, forgetting the history of the last forty years, pin their faith in the maintenance of world peace upon a strengthening of the British Empire. There is, without question, still a considerable latent power in the Empire, but it can only be vitalized along the lines of developing democracy. A commonwealth, held together by spontaneous loyalty and a sense of common interest and outlook, remains undoubtedly a force for peace. But a British policy which sacrifices the essential conditions of democratic development for the sake of avoiding all possible risks to existing imperial interests, whether they be oil wells, spheres of influence, or strict control over the natives, is likely to end in disaster. It is not building a permanent peace, but simply delaying the inevitable war. By sacrificing Ethiopia, Spain, China, and Austria in turn, the British have merely maintained a truce. This truce permits the dictators to entrench themselves further and to strengthen their position for the eventual showdown.

The Lesson of Napoleon

On November 27, 1792, the French armies seized the duchy of Savoy. Breaking all rules of international comity, the French revolutionaries had interpreted as a free pass to military invasion their resolve to "grant fraternity and assistance to all people who wish to recover their liberty." To give the French an excuse, a group of revolutionaries in a certain region would start an agitation. (The process closely resembles Hitler's and Stalin's methods.) French troops would then occupy the territory. Immediately Jacobin clubs sprang up in the cities. These were composed of French officers and officials as well as revolutionary local citizenry. Sometimes, as in the case of Savoy, an assembly elected at French instigation and under her military protection would request incorporation in France. Thereupon the region would be declared a part of the French Republic. Animated by a fanatic ideology, France was frankly annexationist. Her leaders thought in terms of her "natural frontiers"; like Hitler, they believed that every French-speaking person, indeed every believer in the new revolutionary idea, should be brought within her boundary. Naturally, these procedures aroused profound apprehensions everywhere. In England it was widely believed that the process might even be extended to her own land. Yet, then as now, England was slow in responding to the danger which international anarchy spelled for her.

It was only after Napoleon had stepped forward and through his actions clearly revealed the imperialist sequence of the "ideas of 1789" that Britain took up the challenge. Eight years after the seizure of the French borderlands, Charles James Fox spoke in the House of Commons in a famous debate, as an Englishman may well find himself obliged to speak a few years from now. He was attacking the Tory policy of neutrality.

"All the pretended and hypocritical sensibility for the 'rights of nations and for social order' . . . cannot impose upon those who will take the trouble to look back to the period when this sensibility ought to have aroused us into seasonable exertions [namely the time of the annexation of the Netherlands, Savoy, etc.]. At that time the right honorable gentleman makes it his boast that he was prevented, by a sense of neutrality, from taking any measures of precaution on the subject. . . ." (February 3, 1800.)

By 1800 Britain was locked in a life-and-death struggle with Napoleon which she had to carry on for fifteen more bitter years, often coming close to the very brink of disaster. William Pitt, who was "the right honorable gentleman" to whom Fox referred, had become resolute in his determination to check and destroy French imperialism by all available means. Angered by the opposition, who were pressing him to say what the purpose of this war was, Pitt bitterly denounced Bonaparte, dwelling on his perfidy and rapacity. Peace, he said, was impossible with such a man. He refused to sacrifice real peace by grasping at the shadow when the reality was not within his reach.[10] There are times when there can be no peace no matter how much you may want it. Pitt recalled Cicero's famous Philippic exclamation: "Why do I not want such a peace? Because it is perfidious, because it is dangerous, because it really cannot be."[11] Yet, must not the position of democracy be different? Pitt, after all, was fighting for an empire, and so was Cicero. Under the battle cry of re-establishing the balance of power, the great coalition

[10] See J. Holland Rose, *Life of William Pitt,* part II, p. 385.
[11] *Quia non volo pacem? Quia est perfida, quia periculosa, quia esse non potest.* 7th Philippic.

was organized which brought Napoleon to his knees. That coalition meant war, not peace. Hence, men animated by the democratic spirit cannot lightly follow these counsels. For that spirit is the courageous spirit of real peace, celebrated in the Sermon on the Mount. Blessed are the peace-loving.

Conclusion

What, then, shall be done? From the analogy of 1914 it is argued that America should keep out of this witches' caldron. But events have shown that a policy based on that comparison does not work. The nature of the present conflict makes it impossible to keep out of it. Yet where is there an alternative action promising success? The attempt to organize international solidarity through the League failed. Efforts to strengthen the League by a realistic balancing of powers within and around the League likewise miscarried, after a brief span of success. The permanent sources of conflict were rooted in popular needs which no such machinery was able to cope with. More recently, reliance upon empire as the guardian of a new *pax Britannica* has revealed itself as illusory. Empires are too vulnerable in this age of ideological wars and the revolt of the masses. An empire may need peace, but it cannot bring it. It is not ruled according to the glorious formula of Abraham Lincoln. Hence, it cannot fight for the common people without equivocation. That is the reason why following the British will never do as a rule for American foreign policy. The American people cannot be asked to rescue the British Empire.

Is there, then, no hope? No hope for peace? If one does not willfully shut one's eyes to the course of events since 1919, one must conclude that the only hope for peace lies in the hope of victory—victory of the democratic way of life. By taking peace for granted, the world has drifted into war without realizing what was happening. Hope lies beyond the war which is being fought at present. And it can come true only if the ideas of democracy triumph. A wise man has remarked that we ought to make democracy safe for the world. This can perhaps best be done by making democracy succeed where others have failed, and may fail again in the future.

The world may be plunged into a long, dark night of fierce struggles between great empires contending for world supremacy. Anyone can redraw the map of the world to suit his fancy, grouping it around centers like Tokyo, Moscow, Berlin, Rome, London, and perhaps even Washington. Out of their contest, one victor may emerge supreme, fulfilling Napoleon Bonaparte's dream. Or, more likely, these empires may devour each other as mankind relapses into barbarism. Even now, quite a few observers have the impression that the policy of conservatives in both England and France is directed toward staging a lethal fight to the finish between Bolshevism and Nazism, between Berlin and Tokyo against Moscow. It sounds as improbable as the fairy tale of the little man in the forest who maneuvered the giants into killing each other. Surely, there is only slight hope that such a war could be "localized." But is there any balance by which the fierce antagonism of Communism and Fascism could be held in equipoise? Does the clever scheme of having Russia and Germany fight each other take sufficient account of the possibility that Germany and Russia might join forces, after some suitable "readjustment of ideology"? It is hard to imagine the kind of world organization which would bring to life a happy family of nations as long as dictatorial megalomaniacs lead nations against each other under rival ideologies. It seems a pipe dream indeed.

Yet where there is life, there is hope. More particularly is there the hope that democracy may win through teaching by example. If the true democracies remain better places in which to live, they will not need any ministries of propaganda to tell the world all about it. Both Stalin and Hitler pay their involuntary respects to the superior value of democracy as a form of life. They both try to make us believe that what they have is the true, the real democracy. While parliamentarism is being denounced, Germany reverberates with the slogan of the *Volksgemeinschaft,* which in its higher aspirations is nothing but democracy as a way of life. The plebiscites which Stalin and Hitler indulge in are desperate efforts to reassure themselves on this score. It may seem rank hypocrisy to anyone familiar with genuine, working democracy. But as a French adage has it: Hypocrisy renders homage to virtue by pretending that it is virtue. For a little while it may be hard to uphold your belief in the ultimate justice of the people. But "is there any better or equal hope in the world?"

TEXT OF STIMSON LETTER AGAINST WAR REFERENDUM

FOLLOWING is the text of the letter of Henry L. Stimson, former Secretary of War and later Secretary of State, opposing the Ludlow resolution for a national referendum on a declaration of war:

To THE EDITOR:
THE NEW YORK "TIMES":

Last February there was introduced into the House of Representatives by Mr. Ludlow of Indiana a joint resolution proposing an amendment to the Constitution of the United States in the following terms:

"Section I. Except in the event of an invasion of the United States or its territorial possessions and attack upon its citizens residing therein, the authority of Congress to declare war shall not become effective until confirmed by a majority of all votes cast thereon in a nation-wide referendum. Congress when it deems a national crisis to exist may by concurrent resolution refer the question of war or peace to the citizens of the United States, the question to be voted on being, 'Shall the United States declare war on ——?' Congress may otherwise by law provide for the enforcement of this section."

Upsetting Precedents

That resolution has now been ordered out of committee by a petition signed by 218 members of the House. This action brings it up for immediate consideration in January.

The enactment of such an amendment would revolutionize our historic and constitutional treatment of the most important function of our foreign relations. The power to declare war is placed by the Constitution in the hands of the representatives of the people in Congress assembled. Historically, that power has been exercised upon the recommendation of the President of the United States, who by the same Constitution is vested with the normal control of our foreign relations, through his appointment of our Ambassadors, Ministers and foreign servants. The war-making power has thus been controlled by a carefully devised system of representative government concentrating responsibility upon those leaders, both executive and legislative, who from their official duties are presupposed to have familiarity with the relations and problems existing between this country and its neighbors. It is based upon the fundamental principle of responsibility in government.

Subject Too Delicate

The adoption of this amendment would take away from this system of responsible representative government the final and effective decision as to war and make it dependent upon the direct action of a population of over 130,000,000 people exercised through a nation-wide referendum. No nation-wide referendum upon any question has ever been held by our government nor has any such system of direct action on such a subject as war been exercised anywhere else by a population of similar size or variety. It is a brand new experiment in the most vital and delicate function that a government can be called upon to perform.

In the second place, if adopted and legally adhered to, it would not only revolutionize and destroy our existing plan for national defense but it would, under the conditions of modern warfare, make any system of national defense much less effective if not almost impossible. This can be easily shown.

Under such circumstances this proposal deserves most serious consideration. It cannot be treated lightly. With the support in the House of Representatives now demonstrated to be behind it, the mere bringing of it forward cannot but seriously affect our national position in the world today. It may be regarded among our neighbor nations as indicating weakness of national policy and behavior at a time when stability and steadfastness are pre-eminently required.

Pesthouses Not Involved

The chief argument on behalf of this measure made by its sponsor, Mr. Ludlow, was that inasmuch as the American people already "can cast their ballots for constables or dogcatchers or on the location of pesthouses or waterworks," and inasmuch as the declaration of war is a much more important function than any of these, therefore they should handle this question in the same manner. The short answer to this is that the comparative importance of the two functions is not the sole criterion of appropriate method.

There are other elements which enter into the question, notably the complexity or difficulty of the proposed decision. It is much simpler to catch dogs or to choose constables than it is to carry on the long, difficult series of negotiations and decisions by which a nation steers its course so as to avoid war and preserve peace, and in the light of which it makes the final fateful decision as to whether the time has come when immediate forceful action is the only way to preserve the nation against a much greater danger later on.

Even in the comparatively simple questions of our individual lives, when we come to the important question of whether we shall submit to a major surgical operation we do not hold a popular referendum among our friends and count noses on the subject; we leave the question to the most responsible and expert surgeon we can find and, trusting in his abundant experience and in the exercise of his proved fidelity and character, we place in his hands the decision whether it is necessary that our body shall be submitted to mortal risk. Responsible representative government is based upon the same fundamental method of choice.

International war is merely the final act of long-drawn-out national policy, the product of many prior decisions and the weighing of many divergent considerations. With these basic considerations the general public in any nation is necessarily unacquainted and nowhere more so than in our own country, buried in its time-honored confidence in its own seclusion. The people who by our Constitution must keep themselves familiar with these questions are the President, the Secretary of State and the members of the respective committees of Congress. They are the experts to whom we have entrusted the guidance of our ship through the many vicissitudes which have led up to the ultimate decision as to war. They are our chosen experts and representatives to whom we have long since entrusted the determining factors of our fate. In making their ultimate decision we cannot overrule them without the gravest risk.

System Satisfactory

Furthermore, when we consider the lessons of the past, we find that in our country this system of responsible representative government in the decision of peace and war has worked very well. Manifestly the two most important considerations in judging the success of a nation's war-making policy are, first, that the government should be extremely conservative in deciding that it must fight, and secondly, that when war becomes inevitable the war should be waged successfully by a united nation.

Fair judgment must admit that both of these conditions have been abundantly satisfied by the working of our present system. Our Presidents have been conspicuously reluctant to recommend war until supported and, indeed, urged by their people. McKinley waited for months; Woodrow Wilson for three years, each in the face of constant provocation and popular pressure. When they finally laid the matter before Congress and Congress acted, they were followed into war by a practically unanimous popular support.

In 1898 the war was fought entirely by volunteers, and many more thousands of men struggled to serve than could be accepted by the government. In 1917 the country cheerfully supported a Selective Service Act, under which 4,000,-000 men were enlisted and 2,000,000 sent overseas with the practically unanimous patriotic backing of the entire country. Judged by these criteria the United States showed a greater unity and patriotism than other countries much closer to the conflict and much more directly endangered.

In short, our present system in these two most vital respects has been successful and effective. Our nation, although unmilitary by nature and unwilling to make the usual preparations for trouble which other nations feel obliged to make, although it has been unwilling to support large armies or heavy expenses in equipment in time of peace, and although traditionally it has kept itself aloof from foreign policies and happenings, yet when our leaders have recommended that war was necessary it has entered war with such unanimity and patriotism as to be uniformly successful.

What is almost equally important in this troubled world, it has thus made such a historic record of both moderation and success as to cause it to be both respected and feared by nations which might otherwise have threatened our peace or interfered with our national policies.

Let us now see what effect the proposed change would have upon this generally successful constitutional system upon which we now depend. The proposal seeks to place certain hard and fast limitations upon the power of our representatives to take warlike action. Under it there must be "an invasion of the United States or of its territorial possessions" and also "an attack upon its citizens residing therein." Its supporters seek to draw a line at the geographical boundaries of our territory and to prescribe that our defense shall not begin until an enemy reaches that line, and furthermore shall have actually attacked our citizens within it. The proposal is apparently based on the assumption that a nation cannot be effectively attacked except by an old-fashioned invasion, and that if we wait until that happens we can still satisfactorily defend ourselves.

Today this is so untrue as to be fantastic. It entirely ignores the power and speed of modern air and naval attack, as well as the fragility of our modern urban construction and economic organization. It would at once terminate the sound system upon which our American national defense has been planned for many years. That plan has recognized the historic desire of our people to devote themselves to peaceful pursuits without being required to keep a large standing army for protection. It has therefore endeavored to keep us free from dangerous neighbors. Since its very foundation our government, having during the Revolution experienced realistically the bitterness of invasion, by every means in its power has endeavored to keep invasion as far away from our shores as possible.

To do this we have made our first line of defense a diplomatic one. It has been drawn by the warnings of our Presidents to other nations that if they got too close to us they would be unwelcome; we should regard it as an unfriendly act. This warning was necessarily backed by the implication of force—that if the warning was disregarded, the transgressor might ultimately find our military forces arrayed against it. The result of this diplomacy has been most potent in protecting us against war.

Monroe Doctrine Effective

For over a century the warning of President Monroe in the Monroe Doctrine has preserved this entire hemisphere from the encroachment of dangerous neighbors. It has been the effective guardian of peace in the Western world. It has never had even a resolution of Congress behind it. Its sanction was the realization by other nations that the President of this country was our leader in foreign affairs and that his military recommendations were uniformly followed by his people. A similar warning was used by President Johnson to drive a French imperialistic adventure out of Mexico in 1866.

Similar warnings have preserved the eastern entrance to the Panama Canal against encroachments into the neighborhood of the Caribbean Sea. President Cleveland used such a warning in 1895 against Great Britain in her dispute with Venezuela. President Theodore Roosevelt subsequently used one when the German fleet visited Venezuela to enforce German policy. In unnumbered cases throughout a hundred and fifty years of our national life, growing stronger as we increased in power, that outer line of diplomatic defense to our national safety has stood to protect us against incipient encroachments which might later become threatening.

Mr. Ludlow's proposal would at one blow demolish the efficacy of that front line. It would be taken as a notice to all the world that this people would not fight until long after such outer defenses had been broken through and an actual physical invasion of our own territory had been begun. It would indicate that any statements to the contrary by our Presidents could be safely disregarded by venturesome Powers.

Our second historic line of defense has been the American Navy. Unlike the army, which in peacetime is regularly reduced to a skeleton organization, our policy has been to keep the navy ready for immediate action. Cooperating with it now is our air force, also supposed to be in constant readiness. The chief purpose of this readiness is the same as that behind our diplomatic line—namely to keep all enemies at a safe distance from our shores. Its chief function is to save us from the kind of an attack which Mr. Ludlow's amendment would permit—namely, a sudden surprise offensive by air and sea against the populous cities of our coasts.

And for the benefit of any reader who may not have kept in close touch with the facts and dangers of modern war offensives, let me say that under modern conditions a hostile expedition which had defeated or evaded our navy and approached within 200 miles of our coast, not only could within twenty-four hours strike a devastating blow upon one of our great cities and its neighboring industrial centers, but could within a week thereafter land a hostile force of at least a hundred thousand men upon our shores. To meet such an invasion our present regular army, collecting all its mobile elements from the various quarters of the continent, could not be counted upon to assemble more than 60 to 70 per cent of this number or to do it until after the hostile force was ashore and ready. The National Guard could not be even assembled, let alone organized into tactical units, disciplined and equipped, for many weeks later.

Delayed Defense

To support this outer protective line of our naval defense we have dug and fortified the Panama Canal so that our combined fleet can act in either ocean, and we have also constructed the powerful naval base at Hawaii. Within the semicircle formed by the supporting points of Panama, Hawaii and Alaska, at a distance of more than 2,000 miles from the mainland of the continent, our fleet is now ready to operate as a defense against a western attack. But with all our ships and guns and planes in readiness, if this amendment passes, the signal to fire could not legally be given even should a hostile expedition enter the circle with aircraft carriers and airplanes ready for action against our cities!

It is idle to say that I am citing an absurd illustration which could never actually take place; that even if such a hostile approach should occur no President would permit the letter of a constitutional amendment to deter him from taking defensive action. Such argument ignores the basic vice and poison of the Ludlow proposal. The destructive effect of such a proposal would be felt long before the moment of action. Its presence in our Constitution would hamstring the long course of preparation upon which our present defensive policy is based and upon which our outer line has been resting. It would encourage those who would cut the necessary appropriations for our navy and our air force. It similarly would reduce the necessary equipment and garrison of our outer fortresses. It would destroy the initiative and spirit of our personnel. It would set in motion a long process of deterioration and decay which would ultimately make our present plan entirely impossible. The fundamental policy behind the amendment is basically inconsistent with the fundamental policy of our present defense. The one could not be adopted without destroying the other.

I have thus far spoken only of the material and mechanical aspects of the proposal. Its greatest evils would be its psychical effects upon our people themselves.

Psychical Influences

When a nation faces the mortal test of war, those psychical elements constitute the most important factors in its chances of success. The influence of our country and the respect with which it has been held by some of its most important neighbors in the world have been based upon the patriotism of its people; upon their unity and loyalty and the efficacy with which they have in the past proved ready to follow their leader when necessity arose. Those qualities, inherent in our individual citizens, have been fostered in time of war by our present system of leadership embodied in our system of representative government.

As I have already said, we gave a fine example of it in our mobilization and campaign during the Great War. Consider what the effect upon such superb unity of spirit would be if the methods of Mr. Ludlow's proposal were substituted for our time-honored methods of the past. Instead of being trained to look forward in such a matter to the guidance of our responsible leaders, obliterating all thought of party and faction when once our President and Congress had spoken, we would at that very moment be thrown into the politics of a nation-wide referendum.

On the one side there would be destroyed the terrific and sobering sense of responsibility which now rests upon the President when he makes his recommendation for war, of which Mr. Wilson so eloquently spoke in his war address to Congress in April, 1917. In its place the President would be forced to consider the arts and machinations of the political leader and the methods necessary to a high pressure mass appeal. On the other side the people would be diverted from their consideration of the national purpose involved in the President's recommendation and would be distracted by the lower appeals and cross-currents put forward by every kind of selfish leader or faction for every conceivable political purpose.

Divided Support

At best, when the referendum was over, the President would have behind him the support of a people temporarily delayed and distracted by irrelevant local appeals. At worst we might enter the war with a popular support which had been openly divided and weakened in the face of our enemy. No more effective engine for the disruption of national unity on the threshold of a national crisis could ingeniously have been devised. On the most charitable supposition it could only have been brought forward in an atmosphere of complete detachment from the realities of the modern outside world and from experience with the necessities of a successful national defense.

Not for a moment is this warning to preserve our national security to be taken as a counsel of despair by any earnest worker for peace. For many years in public and private life I have supported the effort by co-operative action among the nations to establish a reign of law and respect for treaties under which the peaceful settlement of controversies should eventually supplant the rule of force. I believe that ultimately such a reign of law will be established, and furthermore I believe that it will begin with the co-operative action of those nations which, like ourselves, have already become habituated to the practice of self-government at home and self-control abroad.

Disturbing Period

At present we are faced with a period of world unsettlement which, although we are confident that it is transitory, is nevertheless profound and disturbing. A spirit of violence and disregard for treaty obligations is abroad, and although the governments to which it is confined are few in number, they are powerful. Our first duty must be to preserve the safety of our own civilization and the traditions of law and liberty within our own borders. Upon our experience at home with these traditional principles depends our confidence in the same principles for security throughout the international field. Confidence and strength within our own borders will also render the most effective encouragement to those other nations whose aims are similar to our own.

Each liberty loving and self-governing nation which in

the turmoil of the present stands serene in its own strength and loyal to its principles becomes today a veritable "strong-point" of defense in a troubled world. Between it and its steadfast neighbors can then be begun again the common structure of international law and security for the future. It is not the time for the exhibition of untried panaceas or any other evidence of instability of purpose. Quiet confidence in our own principles and institutions, coupled with ability to repel attacks on our own peace, are the stepping stones at present toward the ultimate goal for which we all pray.

HENRY L. STIMSON.

New York, Dec. 21, 1937.

APPENDIX II

HULL'S ADDRESS OUTLINING FOREIGN POLICY OF THE UNITED STATES

Special to The New York *Times*

WASHINGTON, March 17 (1938).—The address of Cordell Hull, Secretary of State, before the National Press Club today was as follows:

In the course of the daily press conferences at the Department of State I have occasion to see many of you and to touch upon day-to-day developments in our foreign relations. Such information as I am able to give you in these conferences must, of necessity, relate to specific questions and oftentimes, to isolated events. Yet upon you, representatives of the press, rests a heavy responsibility in keeping our people currently and accurately informed on the vital issues which arise in our country's relations with other nations. I welcome, therefore, this opportunity to meet with the members of the National Press Club in the calmer atmosphere of an occasion like the present one, and to discuss with you some of the fundamental conditions and problems presented by our international relations and our foreign policy.

The primary objectives of our foreign policy are the maintenance of the peace of our country and the promotion of the economic, the social and the moral welfare of our people. Unfortunately, the means of attaining these objectives involve today so many factors of great complexity that their real significance is frequently misunderstood and misinterpreted.

By instinct and tradition our country has been throughout its history sincerely devoted to the cause of peace. Within the limitations imposed by time and circumstance, we have earnestly sought to discharge our responsibilities as a member of the family of nations in promoting conditions essential to the maintenance of peace. We have consistently believed in the sanctity of treaty obligations and have endeavored to apply this belief in the actual practice of our foreign relations. In common with all other nations we have, since the end of the World War, assumed a solemn obligation not to resort to force as an instrument of national policy. All this gives us a moral right to express our deep concern over the rising tide of lawlessness, the growing disregard of treaties, the increasing reversion to the use of force and the numerous other ominous tendencies which are emerging in the sphere of international relations.

Recalls Statement Last Year

On July 16, 1937, I issued a public statement, setting forth the fundamental principles to which our government adheres in the formulation of its foreign policy. On behalf of our government, I transmitted a copy of this statement to every government of the world, requesting such comment as each might see fit to offer. To our profound gratification, an overwhelming majority of those governments joined in affirming their faith in these vital principles.

The most important of these principles, which are indispensable to a satisfactory international order, are as follows:

Maintenance of peace should be constantly advocated and practiced.

All nations should, through voluntary self-restraint, abstain from use of force in pursuit of policy and from interference in the internal affairs of other nations.

All nations should seek to adjust problems arising in their international relations by processes of peaceful negotiation and agreement.

All nations should uphold the principle of the sanctity of treaties and of faithful observance of international agreements.

Modification of provisions of treaties, when need therefor arises, should be by orderly processes carried out in a spirit of mutual helpfulness and accommodation.

Each nation should respect the rights of others and perform scrupulously its own established obligations; in brief, international law and the spirit which underlies it must be revitalized and strengthened.

Steps should be taken toward promotion of economic security and stability the world over through lowering or removal of barriers to international trade, according to effective equality of commercial opportunity, and application of the principle of equality of commercial treatment.

National armaments should be limited and be progressively reduced; at the same time, realizing the necessity for maintaining armed forces adequate for national security, each nation should to that end be prepared to reduce or increase its own armed forces in proportion as reductions or increases are made by other nations.

Apart from the question of alliances with others, each nation should be prepared to engage in co-operative effort, by peaceful and practicable means, in support of these principles.

Holds Nations Must Obey Law

The peace and progress of every nation are just as dependent on international law and order, based upon the foregoing principles, as the welfare, stability, and progress of a community are dependent upon domestic law and order, based upon legal, moral, and other recognized standards of conduct. No government faithful to the sacred trust involved in the task of providing for the safety and well-being of its people can disregard these universal principles. Every nation, whatever its form of government, can support them. Every nation must support them, if civilization is to survive. The longer the nations delay acceptance and observance of these fundamental tenets of constructive statesmanship, the graver will be the jeopardy into which all worth-while international relationships will be plunged, and with them the welfare, the happiness, and the civilized existence of all nations.

The crucial issue today is whether these principles will be vitalized and be firmly established as the foundation of an international order, or whether international anarchy based on brute force will inundate the world and ultimately sweep away the very bases of civilization and progress. That issue is universal. No more than a community or a nation, can the world base its existence in part on law and in part on lawlessness, in part on order and in part on chaos, in part on processes of peace and in part on methods of violence.

On August 23 I made another public statement, reaffirming the principles which should underlie international order, peace, and justice, if the world is to avoid a relapse into another dark night of international anarchy and general retrogression.

I called attention again to the fact that if these principles are to be effective they must be universal in their application. This statement was prompted by the fact that the progress and possibilities of armed conflict were becoming more alarming both in the European and the Far Eastern areas, and that the basic principles to which I have just referred were being challenged and the doctrine of armed force was gaining supremacy in important regions of the world.

Appealed to Japan and China

During the early months of the conflict in the Far East I appealed on several occasions, in the name of our Government, to both Japan and China to desist from using armed force and to resort to the well-recognized processes of peaceful settlement for the adjustment of whatever differences existed between them. I said that we would be glad to be of assistance toward facilitating, in any manner that might be practicable and mutually agreeable, resort by them to such processes.

On August 17, and with frequent reiteration thereafter, I stated that we did not intend to abandon our nationals and our interests in China.

From time immemorial, it has been the practice of civilized nations to afford protection, by appropriate means and under the rule of reason, to their nationals and their rights and interests abroad. This policy has been pursued by the Government of the United States throughout the existence of our country.

Methods and means of affording protection abroad vary according to the places in which and the circumstances under which protection is called for. In the case of China, where unusual local conditions were such that the protection afforded by local authorities did not suffice to give security against excited and lawless elements, there have occasionally been sent—not by this country alone but by a number of countries—armed forces, to contribute to the affording of such protection as is due under the rules of international law and the provisions of treaties. American forces thus sent to China have at no time had any mission of aggression, and it has been the practice of the American Government to withdraw such forces whenever and as soon as the local situation so develops as to warrant the view that their withdrawal can be effected without detriment to American interests and obligations in general.

In announcing our intention to afford appropriate and reasonable protection to our rights and interests in the Far East, I stated clearly that we are fully determined to avoid the extremes either of internationalism or of isolationism. Internationalism would mean undesirable political involvements; isolationism would either compel us to confine all activities of our people within our own frontiers, with incalculable injury to the standard of living and the general welfare of our people, or else expose our nationals and our legitimate interests abroad to injustice or outrage wherever lawless conditions arise.

Ours a Middle Course, He Says

Steering a sound middle course between these two extremes, we are convinced that a policy of affording appropriate protection—under the rule of reason, in such form as may be best suited to the particular circumstances, and in accordance with the principles we advocate—is imperatively needed to serve our national interest.

Our decision in this matter is based not only on what we firmly believe to be a specific and elementary duty of a government toward its citizens, but also on other and broader considerations. Respect by a country for the rights and interests of others is a visible test of the fulfillment of obligations assumed by virtue of acceptance of international law and of undertakings embodied in negotiated international instruments. It is, therefore, a test of the observance of those fundamental principles of civilized relations among nations, which, if firmly established, provide in themselves the best means of protection against violation and abuse of the legitimate rights and interests of every nation.

To waive rights and to permit interests to lapse in the face of their actual or threatened violation—and thereby to abandon obligations—in any important area of the world, can serve only to encourage disregard of law and of the basic principles of international order, and thus contribute to the inevitable spread of international anarchy throughout the world. For this country, as for any country, to act in such manner anywhere would be to invite disregard and violation of its rights and interests everywhere, by every nation so inclined, large or small.

Policy Is Called Traditional

To respect the rights of others and to insist that others respect our rights has been the traditional policy of our country. This policy was admirably expressed by James Monroe when, in his message to Congress on December 2, 1823, he said:

"Our policy . . . remains the same . . . to cultivate friendly relations . . . and to preserve those relations by frank, firm and manly policy, meeting in all instances the just claims of every power, submitting to injuries from none."

In a world in which the rule of force has not as yet been

firmly and surely supplanted by the rule of law, it is the manifest duty of a great nation to maintain armed forces adequate for its national defense. Writing on this subject, which was as vital to our national life 150 years ago as it is today, James Madison said:

"The means of security can only be regulated by the means and the danger of attack. They will, in fact, be ever determined by these rules, and by no others."

It is the duty of the Federal Government to insure the safety of our country and to determine what "means of security" are, at any given moment, needed to provide against "the means and the danger of attack." The responsible heads of our naval establishment offer convincing reasons in support of the program, now before the Congress, to render adequate the means of our national defense. No policy would prove more disastrous than for an important nation to fail to arm adequately when international lawlessness is on the rampage.

It is my considered judgment that, in the present state of world affairs, to do less than is now proposed would lay our country open to unpredictable hazards. It would, moreover, seriously restrict our nation's ability to command, without purpose or occasion for resorting to arms, proper respect for its legitimate rights and interests, the surrender of which would constitute abandonment of the fundamental principles of justice and morality and peace among nations.

Denies Any Alliance

The maintenance of these principles that are of concern to all nations alike cannot and should not be undertaken by any one nation alone. Prudence and common sense dictate that, where this and other nations have common interests and common objectives, we should not hesitate to exchange information and to confer with the governments of such other nations and, in dealing with the problems confronting each alike, to proceed along parallel lines—this government retaining at all times its independence of judgment and freedom of action. For nations which seek peace to assume with respect to each other attitudes of complete aloofness would serve only to encourage, and virtually invite, on the part of other nations lawlessly inclined, policies and actions most likely to endanger peace.

In the present Far Eastern emergency we have consistently collaborated with other peace-seeking nations in the manner I have just described. I have said often, and I repeat again, that in this collaboration there is not a trace of alliance or involvement of any sort. We have scrupulously followed and we intend to follow the traditional policy of our country not to enter into entangling alliances or involvements with other countries.

When the Brussels conference was called this country, as one of the original signatories of the Nine-Power treaty and in accordance with its treaty obligations thus assumed, promptly accepted the invitation to the conference. Our delegation co-operated fully with the representatives of the other conference powers in examining the situation in the Far East and exploring methods of bringing about peace by processes of agreement. The conference made a substantial contribution toward keeping alive principles of world order and of respect for the pledged word. Its declarations placed a new emphasis upon the deep concern of peaceful nations over any developments that threaten the preservation of peace.

In connection with the Far Eastern situation, this government was confronted with the question of applying the existing neutrality legislation, which was designed primarily to keep our nation out of war. After mature deliberation, the conclusion was reached that in the circumstances attending the controversy in the Far East—a type of circumstances which the authors of the legislation could scarcely have visualized—application of the law would be most likely to endanger the very objectives which the law was designed to promote. Accordingly, exercising the discretion vested in him by the law itself, the President has refrained from putting the provisions of that law into operation.

Points to President's Ship Statement

At the same time, in pursuance of our general policy of avoiding unnecessary risks, the President announced, on September 14, 1937, that "merchant vessels owned by the Government of the United States will not hereafter, until further notice, be permitted to transport to China or Japan any of the arms, ammunition or implements of war which were listed in the President's proclamation of May 1, 1937," and that "any other merchant vessels, flying the American flag, which attempt to transport any of the listed articles to China or Japan will, until further notice, do so at their own risk."

Our government pursues, in relation to every world area alike, a policy of non-interference, with ill-will toward no nation and a sincere desire to be friendly with all. At the same time, we endeavor to afford appropriate protection to American citizens and American interests everywhere. During recent months, as throughout the past 150 years, the Government of the United States has sought to exercise moral influence and to co-operate in every practicable way with all peace-seeking nations in support of those basic principles which are indispensable to the promotion and maintenance of stable conditions of peace.

We have affirmed on every possible occasion and have urged upon all nations the supreme need for keeping alive and for practicing sound fundamental principles of relations among civilized nations. We have never entertained and we have not the slightest intention to entertain any such notion as the use of American armed forces for "policing the world." But we equally have not the slightest intention of reversing a tradition of a century and a half by abandoning our deep concern for and our advocacy of the establishment everywhere of international order under law, based upon the well-recognized principles to which I have referred. It is our profound conviction that the most effective contribution which we, as a nation sincerely devoted to the cause of peace, can make—in the tragic conditions with which our people, in common with the rest of mankind, are confronted today—is to have this country respected throughout the world for integrity, justice, goodwill, strength and unswerving loyalty to principles.

The foregoing is the essence of our foreign policy. The record is an open book. We spare no effort to make known the facts regarding our attitude, our objectives and our acts. We are always ready to furnish to the members of the Congress essential information. You, gentlemen, have firsthand knowledge of our constant effort to keep the press and the public informed.

Says Future Cannot Be Charted

There is one thing that we cannot do. And that is to prepare and place before every government of the world a detailed chart of the course of policy and action which this country will or will not pursue under any particular set of circumstances. No man, no nation can possibly foresee all the circumstances that may arise. Moreover, to attempt to make such a detailed chart of future action would merely result in impairing our effectiveness in working for the one objective toward which we constantly strive and on which, I am certain, there is not a vestige of disagreement among the people of our country—the establishment of durable peace.

So strong, indeed, is the desire of this country for peace that many measures have been suggested toward our keeping out of war—some of them in complete disregard of both experience and practicability. It has been urged that we apply the Neutrality Law automatically in all circumstances, without adequate consideration of the possible consequences of such action for our own peace and for the safety of our citizens. It has been urged that we withdraw precipitately from any part of the world in which violators of international decencies choose to assert themselves. It has even been urged that we change the very basis of our representative form of government in a frantic search for something which the proposers assume would make it more likely that this country avoid war.

I take it for granted that all of us alike are sincere friends of peace. This makes it all the more necessary for every one of us to scrutinize carefully every measure proposed, lest in our attempts to avoid war we imperil the chances of preserving peace.

The problem of the form of government best adapted to this country's needs was one with which the founders of our Republic came to grips in those stirring days when the structure of our independent national existence was being given form and substance. After exhaustive deliberation and discussion, they decided upon the system of representative democracy in preference to that of pure democracy as the system through which the people could best safeguard their liberty and promote their national security and welfare. The wisdom of the founders of this nation in deciding, with conspicuous unanimity, to place the conduct of foreign relations in the hands of the Federal Government has stood the test of generations as providing the most effective means that can be devised for assuring the peace, the security, and the independence of our people.

Opposes War Referendum

What warrant is there, in reason or in experience, for the assumption—which underlies such proposals as the plan for a popular referendum on the subject of declaring war—that the Chief Executive and the Congress will be at any time more eager and more likely to embark upon war than would be the general body of citizens to whom they are directly responsible? No President and no Congress have ever carried this country into war against the will of the people. On the other hand, there is not a vestige of doubt that the adoption of a procedure like the referendum plan would hopelessly handicap the government in the conduct of our foreign relations in general and would thus disastrously impair its ability to safeguard the interests of the nation, in the forefront among which is that of peace.

Likewise dangerous, from the viewpoint of the preservation of peace, is the proposal that we retire from the Far East, comprising the chief portion of the Pacific area. Unfortunately, many people in this country have wholly misunderstood the position and policy of our government in relation to that situation.

Some have visualized only our trade and investment relationships with China, or our moral and cultural interests there, symbolized by missionary, educational, medical, and similar activities. Some have concentrated their attention solely upon the incidental and exceptional facts of the existence of extraterritoriality and the maintenance of some armed forces to assist in safeguarding our nationals against possible mob violence and similar disorders—special rights which it is our policy to give up and forces which it is our policy to withdraw the moment the unusual conditions disappear.

All these are important. But the interest and concern of the United States—whether in the Far East, in any other part of the Pacific area, in Europe, or anywhere else in the world—are not measured alone by the number of American citizens residing in a particular country, or by the volume of investment and trade, or by exceptional conditions peculiar to the particular area. There is a much broader and more fundamental interest—which is, that orderly processes in international relationships based on the principles to which I have referred be maintained.

Points to "Contagious Scourge"

As I have already indicated, what is most of all at stake today, throughout the world, is the future of the fundamental principles which must be the foundation of international order as opposed to international anarchy. If we and others were to abandon and surrender these principles in regard to the Pacific area, which is almost one-half of the world, we would have to reconcile ourselves to their certain abandonment and surrender in regard to the other half of the world.

It would be absurd and futile for us to proclaim that we stand for international law, for the sanctity of treaty obligations, for non-intervention in internal affairs of other countries, for equality of industrial and commercial rights and opportunities, for limitation and reduction of armaments —but only in one-half of the world, and among one-half of the world's population. The catastrophic developments of recent years, the startling events of the past weeks, offer a tragic demonstration of how quickly the contagious scourge of treaty-breaking and armed violence spreads from one region to another.

Those who contend that we can and should abandon and surrender principles in one-half of the world clearly show that they have little or no conception of the extent to which situations and developments in any part of the world of today inevitably affect situations and conditions in other parts of the world. The triumph of this seclusionist viewpoint would inescapably carry the whole world back to the conditions of medieval chaos, conditions toward which some parts of both the Eastern and the Western worlds are already moving.

Blind Extremism Condemned

Such is the fate to which extreme isolationists—isolationists at any price—all those who contend that we should neither protest against abuses nor co-operate with others toward keeping principles alive, those who say that under no circumstances should we insist upon any rights beyond our own territorial waters—such is the fate to which blind extremism of this type would consign this country and the world.

The momentous question—let me repeat—is whether the doctrine of force shall become enthroned once more and bring in its wake, inexorably, international anarchy and a relapse into barbarism; or whether this and other peaceful nations, fervently attached to the principles which underlie international order, shall work unceasingly—singly or in co-operation with each other, as circumstances, their traditional policies and practices, and their enlightened self-interest may dictate—to promote and preserve law, order, morality and justice as the unshakable bases of civilized international relations.

We might, if we could reconcile ourselves to such an attitude, turn our backs on the whole problem and decline the responsibility and labor of contributing to its solution. But let us have no illusions as to what such a course of action would involve for us as a nation.

It would mean a break with our past, both internationally and domestically. It would mean a voluntary abandonment of some of the most important things that have made us a great nation. It would mean an abject retreat before those forces which we have, throughout our whole national history, consistently opposed.

Security Would Be Menaced

It would mean that our security would be menaced in proportion as other nations came to believe that, either through fear or through unwillingness, we did not intend to afford protection to our legitimate national interests abroad, but, on the contrary, intended to abandon them at the first sign of danger. Under such conditions, the sphere of our international relationships—economic, cultural, intellectual and other—would necessarily shrink and shrivel, until we would stand practically alone among the nations, a self-constituted hermit State.

Thrown back upon our own resources, we would find it necessary to reorganize our entire social and economic structure. The process of adaptation to a more or less self-contained existence would mean less production and at higher costs, lower living standards, regimentation in every phase of life, economic distress to wage-earners and farmers, and to their families, and the dole, on an ever-increasing scale.

All this we would be doing in pursuit of the notion that by so doing we would avoid war. But would these policies, while entailing such enormous sacrifices and rendering the nation more and more decadent, really give us any such assurance?

Reason and experience definitely point to the contrary. We may seek to withdraw from participation in world affairs, but we cannot thereby withdraw from the world itself. Isolation is not a means to security; it is a fruitful source of insecurity.

We want to live in a world which is at peace; in which the forces of militarism, of territorial aggression, and of international anarchy in general will become utterly odious, revolting and intolerable to the conscience of mankind; in which the doctrine of order under law will be firmly established; in which there will no longer be one code of morality, honor, justice and fair play for the individual in his relations with other individuals, and an entirely different code for governments and nations in their relations with each other. We want to live in a world in which fruitful and constructive international relationships can serve as a medium for disseminating throughout the world the benefits of the material, spiritual and moral progress of mankind.

"World at Peace Is Possible"

To that end we will continue to give full and sincere adherence to the fundamental principles which underlie international order; we will continue to urge universal acceptance and observance of these principles; we will continue, wherever necessary and in every practicable and peaceful way, to co-operate with other nations which are actuated by the same desires and are pursuing the same objectives; we will persevere in appropriate efforts to safeguard our legitimate rights and interests in every part of the world; and we will, while scrupulously respecting the rights of others, insist on their respecting our rights.

To that end we will continue to strive, through our reciprocal trade program and through other economic policies, to restore the normal processes and to expand the volume of mutually beneficial trade among the nations which is indispensable to an increase of production, employment, purchasing power and general economic wellbeing here and everywhere; we will continue to promote peace through economic security and prosperity; we will continue to participate in the numerous international scientific, technical and other conferences and collaborative efforts which have been such powerful influences in assisting the stream of new ideas, of new discoveries, of learning and culture, to flow throughout the world, and we will continue to urge other nations to give their support to such policies and efforts.

We believe that a world at peace, with law and justice prevailing, is possible, and that it can be achieved by methods to some of which I have referred. That is the cornerstone of our foreign policy—a policy graphically described by President Roosevelt when he said:

"There must be positive endeavors to preserve peace. America hates war. America hopes for peace. Therefore, America actively engages in the search for peace."

The objectives of our foreign policy are as easy to grasp as they are fundamental. The means we are using to attain these objectives are the only means approved by reason and by experience. For the sake of the best interests of our people, we must maintain our strength, our courage, our moral standards, our influence in world affairs—and our participation in efforts toward world progress and peace.

Only by making our reasonable contribution to a firm establishment of a world order based on law can we keep the problem of our own security in true perspective and thus discharge our responsibility to ourselves—to America of today and to America of tomorrow. No other course would be worthy of our past or of the potentialities of this great democracy of which we are all citizens and in whose affairs we all participate.

LIBRARY OF
Southern Methodist University
DALLAS, TEXAS

INDEX

N.B. Proper names are indexed whenever mentioned, topical items and countries only when the weight of the discussion seemed to suggest it. An item which occurs in a footnote is indexed with an "n" after the page number. The appendices are not covered by the Index.

LIBRARY OF
Southern Methodist University
DALLAS, TEXAS

Books That Live

The Norton imprint on a book means that in the publisher's estimation it is a book not for a single season but for the years.

W · W · NORTON & CO · INC.
70 FIFTH AVENUE
NEW YORK